How to Invest in Stocks

A Beginner's Guide to Making Money and Managing Risk in the Stock Market

Rodolfo Tello

ISBN-13: 978-1-63387-016-1

Library of Congress Control Number: 2021931210

TABLE OF CONTENTS

INTRODUCTION

How does the stock market work? Is it really possible to profit from stock investing? Can a total beginner succeed in stock market investing? How can I learn the stock market basics? You have probably thought about investing in the stock market and need answers to these and other related questions. While the stock market can be intimidating for beginners, once they learn about it, they realize that it provides a great opportunity to grow their wealth over time, and use it to build the life they want. This book is here to help you on that journey, so let's get started.

The Standard & Poor's Index (S&P 500), which tracks the performance of stocks from five hundred large publicly-traded companies listed on U.S. stock exchanges, is one of the most reliable indicators of stock market trends. According to Macrotrends data, in the last three decades the S&P 500 reported an average annual return of 9.3 percent. The leading year was 1995, when the return was 34.1 percent, followed by 2013, when the annual return reached

29.6 percent. In 2020, the market returns were 16.26 percent, after experiencing and recovering from the dramatic losses caused by the COVID-19 pandemic.

The rate of growth in the market value of stocks, however, is not straightforward. During the last three decades, the market has also displayed negative returns in one of every four years. These happened particularly between 2000 and 2002, with a -15.5 percent average annual return, following the dot-com crash; and during the 2008 financial crisis, when the annual return was down to -38.5 percent.

Even in periods that do not experience such dramatic volatility, stock prices fluctuate on a regular basis, particularly when we look at their short-term performance. An example is provided by Amazon.com (AMZN). In January 2010, this stock opened at an adjusted price of $136.25, and in January 2020, its price was $1,875, showing a profit percentage of 1,276 percent, with a compound annual growth rate of about 30 percent. If we were to take a short-term view, however, the situation would look different. If an investor had bought this stock on September 1, 2018, for $2,027, four months later they would have seen its price drop to $1,346, reflecting a loss of more than 33 percent. Around six months after that, however, the stock had recovered its previous value, opening at $2,026. By the end of 2020, the value of this stock was much higher, trading at prices above $3,300.

This recovery pattern is consistent even during recession times, including the recession caused by the COVID-19 pandemic. On February 20, 2020, the SPDR S&P 500 ETF Trust (SPY), which emulates the performance of the S&P 500 Index, opened at $337. About a month later, its opening price had dropped to $228, displaying a 32 percent decline. Nevertheless, six months after this downtrend started, SPY's price had recovered to its previous $337 level, and by the end of 2020 it was trading at around $372. This situation, based on S&P 500 data, is illustrated in Chart 1.

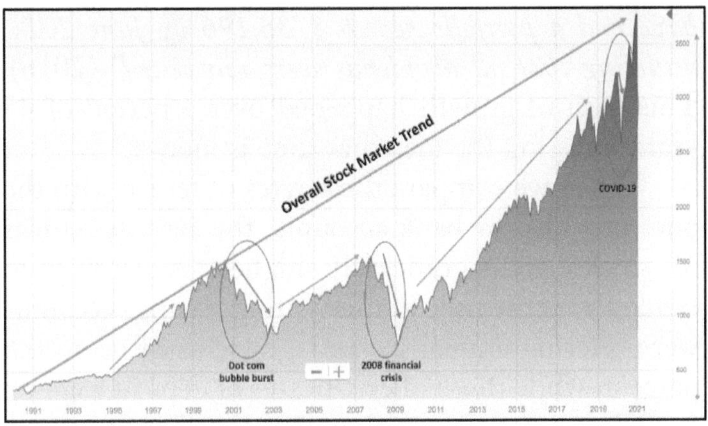

Chart 1. Stock Market Trends in the Last Three Decades

While stock prices experience fluctuations all the time, the overall odds for long-term investors in the stock market are in their favor. As Warren Buffett pointed out, the U.S. stock market prospects over the long term are good, with a market where "*equities will almost certainly outperform cash over the next decade, probably by a substantial degree*," with sound U.S. companies setting new profit records ten and twenty years from now (2008).

This statement is consistent with the information provided by E*Trade, which indicates that "*between*

June 20, 1989 and June 20, 2019 the S&P 500 (SPX) had 4,049 up days and 3,505 down days. That's nearly two more years of 'up' than 'down' out of 30, and if that doesn't sound like much, keep in mind it was enough to produce an 820% rally during that period" (2019).

A similar point was also made by economics professor Burton Malkiel, who explained that "*an investor with $10,000 at the start of 1969 who invested in a Standard & Poor's 500-Stock Index Fund would have had a portfolio worth $736,196 by June 2014, assuming that all dividends were reinvested*" (2016). This level of growth happened over a period of 45 years, stressing the idea that time is money.

When we compare these rates of return with the ones provided by bank accounts, the average returns of stocks are significantly higher. According to Bankrate, at the time of this writing, savings accounts were offering annual percentage yields of up to 0.6 percent, while those of certificates of deposit were up to 0.8 percent for a year (2021). These returns, however, are less than the U.S. annual inflation rate, which in 2020 was 1.4 percent (BLS 2021), and in 2021 is projected to be 2.3 percent (Payne 2021). By holding their cash with the type of returns offered by banks, people's money is actually losing purchasing power parity over time.

Considering this situation, one may wonder why everyone is not investing in stocks. Two important reasons, as Graham (1986) pointed out, are safety, which is associated with the fear that people could lose their hard-earned money, and limited knowledge of how the stock market works, which could be intimidating for beginners without a proper understanding of market volatility.

This book is here to help beginning investors understand how the stock market works, so that they can not only survive but thrive in the stock market. As Kratter (2019) pointed out, "*the stock market is the greatest opportunity machine ever created*," and having a solid foundation can help new investors make informed decisions when investing in the stock market and grow their wealth over time.

The book starts by explaining the characteristics of investment vehicles such as stocks, options, and pooled funds, such as exchange traded funds (ETFs), mutual funds, and index funds, with a focus on stocks and the role of stockbrokers, while briefly discussing other financial securities as well.

The main drivers of change in the price of stocks are addressed next, in the long and short term, including aspects like economic trends and market cycles, business performance and organizational dynamics, the role of policies and politics, and the influence of social factors and the media.

The next chapter explores the main methods to analyze stocks and securities, including fundamental analysis and technical analysis, along with other approaches that combine both of them, plus additional elements to improve investors' chances of identifying stocks with profitable prospects.

The main investment styles are presented after that, providing an overview of approaches like long-term investments, swing trading, and day trading, among other investment strategies.

Managing the risks of investments is covered next, including the importance of adopting a risk management approach throughout the investment process, the basic elements of a risk management methodology, and practical actions that investors can take to protect their stock portfolios.

The importance of investor psychology is also discussed, including the most common emotions faced by investors when facing market volatility, their potential implications on their portfolios, and other areas like investors' attitudes toward timing the markets and investing during recessions.

An introductory chapter on leveraging options investing is also included, explaining the basics of options contracts, calls and puts, pricing indicators, and their potential use by investors.

A hand-picked compilation of resources and tools available for investors is provided next, including online resources such as videos, tools, news, and online training courses, books on stock market investing, financial magazines, and stock advisory services, among many others.

After addressing these topics, the book walks readers through the practical aspects of selecting a stockbroker and opening a brokerage account, understanding order types and situations when they may be used, and discussing the basic elements of an investment plan.

This book was written as an overview for beginning investors to learn how the stock market works, but it is not expected to be a comprehensive study of the topic. Its contents are for educational purposes only and are not intended to be investment, tax, or legal advice. The book neither recommends the purchase or sale of any stock, security, or investment, nor includes the analysis of securities. References to stocks and other securities are included for illustrative purposes only and do not imply an endorsement. Readers interested in investment advice may seek a licensed investment adviser.

This book will not provide readers with recommendations about specific strategies, actions, or steps to follow, either. The reason is that, instead of attempting to replicate other investors' strategies, each investor would be better served by developing an approach that reflects their specific situation, knowledge, experience, and risk tolerance. The focus of the book is on helping beginning investors understand the variety of stock investing alternatives, market scenarios, and tools available for them, giving them the means to carve out their own approach to managing their stock market investments.

The references and assumptions about the stock market refer to the U.S. financial market only. Stock trading activity in other countries may have different assumptions and rules, which readers will need to verify for consistency to avoid potential misunderstandings, as applicable. With these considerations in mind, the next chapter explains the basic characteristics of investing vehicles, including stocks, bonds, index funds, ETFs, mutual funds, options, and futures, among others.

1

INVESTING IN THE STOCK MARKET

When it comes to investors, there are individual investors, accredited investors, and institutional investors. Individual investors, also known as retail investors, are non-professional members of the general population who buy and sell financial securities, usually via an investment account with a stockbroker or via their retirement plans. This book was written for individual investors, so the use of the term *investor* in this book refers mostly to them unless otherwise specified.

Institutional investors are large investing entities like pension funds, mutual funds, insurance companies, investment banks, and hedge funds, among others. There are also accredited investors, who are people or companies with high levels of income, or with a net worth exceeding a million dollars, who can trade securities not registered with the financial authorities. The term investor is usually reserved for those entering the stock market with a long-term horizon. This stands in contrast with traders, which seek to profit from the volatility of the market within shorter time frames.

This chapter explains the basic characteristics of investment vehicles like stocks, options, and pooled funds, such as index funds, mutual funds, and ETFs, focusing on the characteristics of stocks. It also includes brief discussions of other securities that can be traded in stock exchanges, like Nasdaq and the New York Stock Exchange (NYSE), and presents a brief overview of alternative investments.

The term *financial securities* refers to tradable investment vehicles that include equity securities, such as stocks, mutual funds, index funds, and ETFs composed of equity securities; debt securities, like bonds, Treasury bills, and other marketable debt instruments; and derivatives, like options and futures contracts. There are also hybrid debt-equity instruments.

INVESTMENT VEHICLES

Stocks come in different presentations and can be traded in different ways. The most common types discussed in this book are company shares; pooled funds like index funds, mutual funds, and ETFs; and options contracts. These investment vehicles are explained in greater detail next.

Company Shares

This is the typical investment vehicle when we think of stocks. As Bodie et al. explained, stocks are financial assets that represent shares of companies that produce goods and services in the economy and drive revenue from it (2018). The ability of businesses to generate revenue on a continuous basis is crucial; this is why earnings per share (EPS), which public companies release in quarterly earnings reports, are important for investors when determining the valuation of stocks in the market.

Public companies —as opposed to privately held firms not traded on the stock market— are controlled by their boards of directors, whose members are elected by the shareholders based on the number of shares they hold. The ownership of stocks is referred to as having equity in a company.

Company shares are usually bought in whole units, even though some stockbrokers include the possibility to buy fractional shares, or specify a dollar amount that is then converted into shares. This feature can be helpful, for instance, if investors want to buy shares in companies whose stock price exceeds their available budget. Fractional shares also allow investors the opportunity to start purchasing stocks in any company of their choosing with as little as one dollar.

Many companies offer dividends to their shareholders, and most stockbrokers allow investors to automatically reinvest the dividends they receive, in the same company that issued them, instead of receiving those distributions in cash. This helps investors add fractional shares to their portfolios.

Stocks can be located by the tickers assigned to them by the stock exchanges, which can be a combination of letters, numbers, or both. For instance, the ticker AAPL is for Apple Inc., and the ticker Z is for Zillow Group Inc. Index funds, mutual funds, and ETFs also use tickers.

Pooled Funds

The term *pooled funds* refers to groups of stocks that are traded together as a package. The most common types are mutual funds, index funds, and exchange traded funds (ETFs).

Mutual funds invest the combined resources of individual investors. These are open-ended funds that can issue unlimited fund shares to investors. Mutual funds may hold different types of securities in multiple sectors of the market. They usually involve fees, particularly those funds that are actively managed, and those fees could add up over time. Actively managed mutual funds usually have high levels of turnover, making them tax-inefficient vehicles. They also have limitations when it comes to executing buy and sell orders, which is done only once a day, after the market has closed, and investors do not have control over the price at which they get traded. To sell their fund shares at an optimal price, investors would need to find a date when the market is high and place an order that same day, which is not as convenient as placing a trailing or a limit order that can be triggered when the price reaches a certain point, within a specified period, as can be done with stocks and ETFs.

Another popular type of pooled fund is the index fund. The goal of index funds is to match the performance of the index they track. One of their main advantages is the broad diversification they can offer, and since they are not actively managed, their maintenance cost is very low. One of the most common indexes tracked is the S&P 500 index, which covers large-cap (short for market capitalization) companies —those with a comparatively high value on the stock market— but there are also index funds for small-cap and medium-cap companies, as well as total market index funds, which cover all market caps. There are also index funds for bonds and real estate. Index funds do not seek to outperform the markets they track but mimic their return rates instead. See Bogle (2017) for additional details.

Indexes can also help investors understand how the stock market or the economic sectors they track are performing. In addition to the S&P 500 Index, another index is the Dow Jones Industrial Average, which reflects trends in a sample of thirty large publicly traded companies in different sectors of the economy, not just the industrial one. The Nasdaq Composite Index is also a helpful market indicator, particularly for technology companies. Likewise, the Russell 2000 Index is a good indicator of small-cap companies, which are those with a relatively lower market capitalization. The CBOE Volatility Index (VIX) is also important since it provides an indication of levels of fear among investors. While indexes use point systems to track their movement, a practical way investors can interpret their movement is by looking at their percentage of change. They show gains in green and losses in red, so a quick look at their colors can tell us the direction the stock market is going.

Another key investment vehicle is exchange traded funds (ETFs). This is a highly versatile vehicle that can be traded in the same way as stocks, focusing on specific types of companies or sectors of the economy, or including exposure to broader sets of securities. They usually have low fees, and can also allow compositions similar to those of index funds. Investors can trade options on ETFs, short them, or buy fractions of them. The holdings of an ETF package can be reviewed by investors, and many ETFs pass on the dividends issued by the underlying companies to investors. There are also growth ETFs, designed to outperform the market, as well as leveraged, contrarian, real estate, gold, commodity, and many other types of ETFs. Some of them are diversified and others are non-diversified. In sum, ETFs offer great flexibility to accommodate investors' preferences.

One advantage of ETFs over mutual funds is that ETFs do not have the short-term redemption fees that many mutual funds impose on investors if they decide to trade them before a certain period. Even when the funds do not have fees associated with early withdrawals, some stockbrokers impose fees to discourage their frequent trading. In addition, some mutual funds have minimum investment amounts, and they normally have higher management fees than ETFs.

There are also specialized funds, such as real estate investment trusts (REITs). The portfolio of REITs is based on real estate (equity funds) and loans secured by real estate (mortgage trusts). The real estate owned is usually leased, and those proceeds generate dividends. REITs are required by law to give back at least 90 percent of their net earnings as dividends to their shareholders.

Other types of funds include hedge funds, which are available to accredited and institutional investors, structured as private partnerships, where fund managers invest the pooled assets of investors. These are subject to less regulation, which enables them to pursue investment strategies with higher levels of risk. There are also commingled funds, closed-end funds, and others.

Options Contracts

Options contracts are derivative financial products —those that derive their value from the performance of the underlying securities— that can be applied to different investment vehicles, including stocks and ETFs, and can be used as an extension of stock trading strategies. Given the specificity of options, and the different types of options trades available, options are discussed later in a separate chapter. However, something important for options investors to have in mind from the onset is that options have an expiration date, and need to be sold or exercised before they expire; otherwise, they will become void and lose all their value.

Characteristics of Stocks

The term *stocks* is used to refer to the shares of publicly listed companies in stock exchanges like the NYSE and Nasdaq, but in many cases its use is also extended to refer to the stocks in pooled funds such as ETFs and mutual funds.

There are common stocks —those traded in the stock exchanges, which enable shareholders to vote to elect their boards of directors, which hire the executive managers of the underlying companies. There are also preferred stocks, which are given preference when a company is paying dividends and in case of company liquidations.

The main two types of common stocks are growth stocks and value stocks. Growth stocks derive their value from the expected increase in their value over time, which is often related to the level of earnings that can be anticipated by its business operations. For the most part, they do not pay dividends, and they are often expected to outperform the average returns of broad market indexes.

Value stocks are usually those of companies considered to be trading below their intrinsic value, based on the analysis of their earnings, debt, distributions, and other company fundamentals. They are not necessarily expected to show significant growth in the price of their stock over time, but are often a regular source of dividends, which acts as an incentive that attracts investors.

Information on dividends is often a key variable that investors pay attention to. As Ross et al. explain, dividends represent a return on the capital contributed by the shareholders to a corporation, at the discretion of its board of directors, which are paid out of the company's after-tax profits, and are taxable for investors receiving those dividends (2019: 253).

There are also defensive stocks, which are usually those of the larger, older, and established companies with regular cash flows. They are considered less subject to the volatility of the market and are expected to perform better at holding their value during stock market declines.

When privately held companies go public in the stock market, they issue stocks in an initial public offering (IPO), which enables investors to purchase their shares. This is normally achieved with the help of underwriters and investment bankers. Since these shares are sold first to large institutional investors, usually at a discounted price, the initial release of new stocks into the market may present significant levels of volatility (Bodie et al. 2018). There is also a lock-up period for company insiders and some early private investors, who can only sell their shares at the end of this period, which usually lasts for three to six months after a firm goes public.

Companies are classified according to their market capitalization, which is calculated by multiplying the price of their stock by the number of outstanding shares. While there is no official consensus on the cutoff values, small-cap companies typically have a market capitalization between $300 million and $2 billion, and present a higher level of risk than the larger and more established companies. Mid-cap companies have a market capitalization between $2 and $10 billion, while large-cap companies have a market cap of more than $10 billion, with the latter deemed to be less risky and more likely to pay dividends (Chen 2019). Other less-common terms are mega-cap, micro-cap, and nano-cap.

Stocks trade during weekdays only. The hours of operation of the U.S. stock market on regular trading days are Monday to Friday, from 9:30 a.m. to 4:00 p.m., Eastern Time. The stock exchanges are closed on national holidays, and also close early (at 1:00 p.m.) on certain days before or after the holidays.

Stockbrokers usually allow extended trading, which includes pre-market and after-hours trading.

Pre-market trading can start earlier than the regular trading hours, even though it varies according to the stockbroker. E*Trade, for instance, allows pre-market trading starting at 7:00 a.m., Ally Invest at 8:00 a.m., and Robinhood at 9:00 a.m. After-hours trading typically goes from 4:00 p.m. to 8:00 p.m., but for many stockbrokers, this period ends earlier, like at 6:00 p.m.

Alternative Products

While this book is about stocks, it is also important to become familiar with other investment vehicles and financial products, particularly because of the interactions between them. If investors feel that the stock market will be going down, for instance, some of them may liquidate part of their stock positions and purchase bonds, precious metals ETFs, or futures contracts instead, as a precautionary measure aimed at protecting their investment capital from stock price declines.

Most investors interested in stocks are probably familiar with financial products like savings accounts and certificates of deposit offered by commercial banks. They provide a high level of safety for cash funds, since the funds deposited in those institutions are usually backed by insurance provided by the Federal Deposit Insurance Corporation (FDIC), a federal agency that protects customers against the loss of deposit accounts in FDIC-insured banks, up to its current limit of $250,000 per account holder per insured bank. Holding cash reserves can be a strategy for investors who are unsure about the potential direction of the market or who expect imminent market price drops.

Another important category of securities is bonds. These can be government-backed securities and corporate bonds. Bonds issued by governments usually have a maturity period of ten to thirty years (those with ten years or less to maturity are called Treasury notes). Bonds provide a semi-annual coupon payment, which is doubled to calculate the annual yield of the bond. Other types of government-backed securities include Treasury Inflation Protected Securities (TIPS), international bonds, and municipal bonds, among others. Two practical ways to buy bonds in the stock market are through bond mutual funds and bond ETFs, which offer the benefit of holding collections of different bonds. The potential use of bonds in an investment strategy is discussed in chapter 9, particularly in the section about asset allocations.

Corporate bonds allow private companies to borrow money from the public. These include secured bonds (which have some collateral backing them), and unsecured bonds (those with no collateral). There are investment-grade bonds, those of firms that have been assessed and deemed as having the capacity to repay their loans, which can present themselves as safer and offer lower yields. There are also non-investment-grade bonds, sometimes referred to as junk bonds or high-yield bonds, which are highly speculative, and normally need to offer higher yields to attract investors willing to take higher levels of risk. Bond ratings are issued by agencies such as Standard & Poor's, Moody's, and Fitch.

Commodity futures also represent an important investment vehicle. They are based on derivative contracts to buy a certain commodity by a given time in the future, at a predetermined price, regardless of the price of that product in the market at that time. The buyer of a futures contract must buy the asset when the contract expires, but investors usually sell their contracts to others who will eventually take possession or use the product specified in the contract. Examples of commodities traded in the futures market include agricultural products (corn, wheat, coffee, sugar, cotton), energy (oil barrels, gasoline, natural gas), and metals (gold, silver, copper). The trends in the first session of futures contracts in the week, which opens on Sunday at 6:00 p.m. EST, sometimes can be an indicator of sentiment regarding stock prices the next day. Futures trading involves a higher level of risk. People interested in learning more about futures, along with examples of trading strategies for this type of derivative contract from a trader's perspective, may find it useful to read the book *Mastering the Trade* (Carter 2012).

The exchange of foreign currencies (forex) is another trading activity, which, depending on the movement of currency pairs in the international market, can produce profits for traders. It includes forward market and futures market contracts, and the spot market, which is based on cash transactions and is where most retail traders conduct their exchange activities. The trading of currencies is a speculative activity, conducted based on the analysis of the socio-economic factors that could affect the supply and demand balance of a pair of currencies. The forex market is open twenty-four hours a day, five and a half days per week (from 5:00 p.m. EST on Sunday to 4:00 p.m. on Friday). Forex trading involves a high level of risk.

Cryptocurrencies have also been on the radar of some investors, particularly because of their rapid increase in value. This happened mostly between November 2013, when Bitcoin (BTC) hit the $1,000 mark, and December 2017, when its value exceeded $19,000. After that, BTC started a quick decline, with its price falling below $4,000 in 2018. In 2020, however, its value recovered from its previous downtrend, with its trading price exceeding $23,000, and at the beginning of 2021 it had reached new highs, trading at over $50,000. Other cryptocurrencies also experienced substantial levels of growth and decline. This level of growth attracted many people interested in speculating on even further price gains. Cryptocurrencies trade in specialized platforms, like Coinbase Pro, Bittrex, and Kraken. Some stockbrokers like Webull, Robinhood, eToro, and Sofi Invest also offer the option to invest directly in cryptocurrencies, while many other stockbrokers allow Bitcoin trusts and futures trading. Because of its huge level of volatility, this is a speculative activity with a particularly high level of risk. There are also cybersecurity risks, as evidenced by the many hacking incidents involving the theft of data affecting cryptocurrency holders, service providers, and other market participants.

2

WHAT DRIVES THE PRICE OF STOCKS?

Stock price changes in the market are driven by multiple factors that affect the supply and demand for the shares of a company or other financial securities. If there are more buyers than sellers, the prices will go up, and the inverse will happen if there are more sellers than buyers.

This happens because the stock market functions through a bid system. When many investors want to buy a stock at the same time, the ones with the highest bids get their orders filled first, and as long as there are more buyers than sellers, the price of the stock goes up in every iteration. Conversely, when many investors compete to sell their shares, every trade drives prices further down. This happens because stock trading is affected by the economic principle of scarcity, which creates a form of rivalry between buyers and sellers, between buyers, and between sellers (Baye and Prince 2017).

Accordingly, stock price movements are ultimately determined by the aggregated decisions that investors make regarding the buying, holding, and selling of stocks at any given time. The price of stocks shown in financial tables and charts is the temporary display of the last recorded transaction.

The decisions of investors are shaped by a variety of factors that affect their perceptions of what may happen in the market, which eventually leads to bull or bear markets. According to the Securities and Exchange Commission (SEC), a bull market happens when investors are optimistic that the price of stocks will go up, with stock prices rising by at least 20 percent in a broad market index over a period of at least two months. Conversely, a bear market refers to times when stock prices decline and market sentiment is pessimistic, when a broad market index falls by 20 percent or more over at least a two-month period.

The following sections explain how stock prices are affected by economic trends and market cycles, business performance and organizational dynamics, the role of policies and politics, and the influence of social factors, including media channels and other communication outlets. The collective influence of investors' psychology is also relevant, but this topic is addressed in a separate chapter.

ECONOMIC TRENDS

Key topics in the analysis of economic trends, which reflect the conditions in which the business operations of the companies whose shares trade in the stock market take place, include a broad understanding of market cycles, country projections, sector trends, and disruptive technologies.

Market Cycles

The stock market experiences economic trends with different time frames, displaying expansions in some periods and contractions in others. According to the method developed by Richard Wyckoff, as explained by Farley (2020), stock market cycles are characterized by the following four stages:

1. Accumulation stage, when the market is at its bottom level, after experiencing a decline, with some investors starting to buy stocks at discounted prices in relation to their previous highs
2. Markup stage, when larger numbers of investors buy stocks, so their prices display a growing trend, which continues as long as there are more buyers than sellers
3. Distribution stage, when the investors who bought stocks during the accumulation or markup stage start selling their positions
4. Markdown stage, when the stock prices show a downtrend, once there are considerably more sellers than buyers in the market, until the market bottoms out and a new cycle starts

Chart 2 illustrates the application of these four stages in a graphic format. Additional information about this approach can be found in the book *How I Trade and Invest in Stocks and Bonds* (Wyckoff 1925). The Wyckoff Stock Market Institute also offers online courses for beginners based on this approach.

In this framework, the best time to buy stocks is during the accumulation phase, even though in practice most of the buying transactions happen during the markup and distribution stages. When large numbers of investors who bought stocks during the accumulation and markup stages consider that the market has reached, or is close to reaching its top levels, they begin selling their stocks, starting the distribution stage. By that time, the rising price of the stocks experienced during the markup stage makes it easy for the early investors to find new buyers who consider that the recent uptrend in stock prices is likely to continue. However, when the number of sellers exceeds the number of buyers, the price of stocks drops down until the point where more investors start buying again.

Regarding the timing of these cycles, it changes depending on varying circumstances, with some cycles being stronger and lasting longer than others. From a historical perspective, the more pronounced bear markets have occurred every 3.5 years or so, as reported by McAllen (2012), and when they happened, they lasted for about 1.7 years to get back to breakeven status.

The main difficulty associated with the analysis of market cycles, however, is that in most cases it is very difficult to predict when the next stage in a cycle will happen, particularly when the market has reached its accumulation and its distribution stages. Retrospective analyses can show signs that such changes were coming more clearly than at the time those events happened.

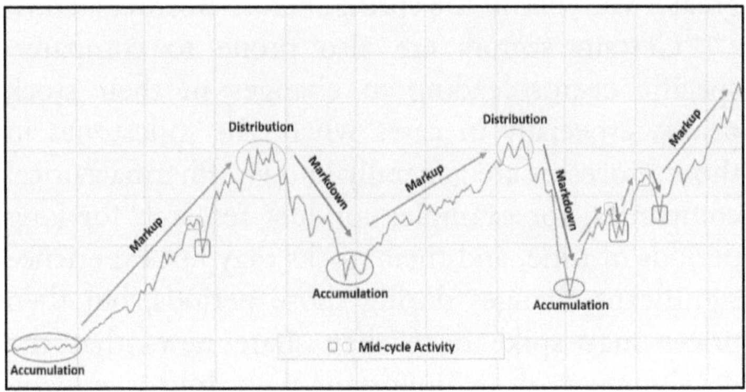

Chart 2. Stages in the Market Cycle

Even the ones who identify the market trends correctly will be taking the risk that they may be misjudging the situation, and the risk of not seeing the trends consolidate within their forecasted time frames. Such investors would need to be comfortable adopting a contrarian approach, to be able to start buying when most investors think the best course of action is still selling, and vice versa.

It is also important to notice that the price of stocks between one cycle and another may be different, so rather than focus on price comparisons, it is the conditions associated with each stage that would be most relevant for market cycle analyses.

There are also seasonal patterns that are normally considered when assessing market trends. For instance, sports and ice cream companies are more likely to sell their goods during the summer season, while retailers are most likely to show profits after the winter holidays, like Christmas. Candy producers will see more sales in the fall, particularly prior to

Halloween, while jewelry sales may experience greater volumes in the spring, before Mother's Day.

Certain sectors are also prone to company-specific events leading to changes in their stock prices, especially in cases where the milestones in those processes are generally known. Pharmaceutical companies, for example, conduct research for long periods of time, and their stocks may not experience significant changes during those periods, but then prices may spike once they share news that the development of an important new drug is moving forward, like when a company announces the start of human trials, when it files for federal approvals, or when approvals are granted, among others.

Large purchases by institutional investors also affect stock prices. Because of the heavy volume of purchases and sales institutions normally conduct, market prices experience increased levels of demand that can drive prices higher when they are buying. The opposite happens when they are selling their stocks, with prices going down as such large numbers can flood the market. These market transactions can be gradual and happen over days, weeks, and even months (Bodner and Downey 2020).

Economic analyses also need to take into account the potential disruptions to market cycles caused by black swan events and recessionary periods, like those caused by the COVID-19 pandemic, and even after these events pass, the restrictions lift, and the economy gets gradually back to normal, the new normal may have significantly different characteristics than the original one.

Country Projections

Long-term projections for the larger economies can set the context for investors to feel more or less optimistic about global market trends. According to the World Economic Forum, based on the analysis of gross domestic product data, China could displace the United States from its top place in the global economy as early as 2024. India, Indonesia, and Russia are also poised to move up in the world economic ranking, while the UK, France, Germany, and Japan are expected to slide down (Buchholz 2020). These trends may influence some investors' decisions regarding stocks from companies in these countries.

Country-specific macroeconomic factors may be relevant to consider as part of the analysis as well, including monetary policies, inflation, levels of debt, monetary reserves, trade agreements, and credit risk ratings, among others. These can affect areas like interest rates, exchange rates, bond rates, and futures contracts, which in turn can have an effect on the price of stocks.

When conducting this type of analysis, it would be important to remember that we live in a global economy, and as a result, country trends can be better understood in the context of their interactions with other countries and economic blocs. Participation in bilateral and multilateral trade agreements make a difference in the trading conditions and can shape future economic trends.

Considering that many U.S. companies rely heavily on overseas primary suppliers, the conditions and risks associated with the countries where their manufacturing or production processes happen can also be important to consider. The location of the customers that buy the products and services offered by a company may also be relevant. An Israeli firm, for instance, may have outsourced most of its production to subcontractors in China and serve mostly clients in the United States, Canada, Australia, and Europe.

An important metric that often influences U.S. stock prices, not just the shares of individual companies but the market in general, is related to unemployment rates. This effect is based on the Employment Situation Summary, an economic news release issued by the Bureau of Labor Statistics on the first Friday of every month. This indicator is particularly relevant during recessions, along with related job-related figures such as the number of people applying for unemployment benefits.

While some of these macroeconomic trends by themselves may not lead to direct investment decisions, in many cases they prepare the stage for investors' reactions to events in ways shaped by those trends, particularly if they confirm their perceptions or concerns. For instance, when analysts and the media start reporting that the banks in a country known for its strong financial sector may be now struggling, investors may be more likely to sell those positions if such news is interpreted as confirmation of their larger economic concerns, increasing the number of sellers in the market.

Sector Trends

The trends affecting a given economic sector are an important factor to consider. For instance, investors convinced that the future of home entertainment will be dominated by Internet TV and wireless communications, with online streaming gradually replacing wired cable programming and other conventional technologies, may consider that the stocks of traditional providers have limited potential to grow or sustain the ability to issue the same level of dividends over time.

In a similar way, e-commerce has been gaining greater market share in many segments traditionally dominated by brick-and-mortar stores, and that trend has even intensified during the COVID-19 pandemic, forcing many firms to go bankrupt. Companies that filed for Chapter 11 bankruptcy in 2020 include JCPenney, Pier 1, GNC, California Pizza Kitchen, JoS. A. Bank, Lord & Taylor, Century 21, and Ruby Tuesday, among many others.

The changing size of the market in a given sector is another factor to consider, since it is not only market share percentage that counts, but also whether trends in the sector indicate if the demand for a given industry is likely to grow or shrink. The coal industry, for instance, may see its levels of demand gradually shrink as the use of renewable energy sources increases, while the business opportunities for renewable energy companies are likely to grow (Howe 2004).

This scenario sets the stage for investors to become cautious about companies in struggling sectors, with many investors getting ready for opportunities to divest those positions, if they have them, or look at alternative options to invest instead. If enough investors stop buying shares of companies in those sectors, fewer buyers than sellers can make their stock prices eventually go down, affecting even companies in the affected sectors whose financials are doing well.

Disruptive Technologies

The rise of cryptocurrencies introduced a new scenario with different rules than the ones for traditional investments. They started without being subject to regulatory controls, even though many governments have been increasingly passing new regulations on this activity.

One of the main differences between cryptocurrencies and stocks is that there is no underlying company as the basis for the valuation of cryptocurrencies, whose price is determined by their users, based on their aggregated expectations of growth or decline. Their valuation is guided by supply and demand, so fundamental notions such as intrinsic value do not apply to them. However, if enough users were to adopt cryptocurrencies for business transactions, it is possible to envision a scenario where some resources from the stock market could be moved to cryptocurrency markets. While the market capitalization of cryptocurrencies at the time of this writing is still not large enough to induce substantial changes in the stock market, this situation could change in the future.

While speculative, many people have adopted cryptocurrencies as an alternative form of investment, in similar ways as buying precious metals, jewelry, art, collectible items, etc. In that sense, a cryptocurrency market crash could trigger massive selling activity, and those proceeds may be used to buy stocks. If the movement were strong enough to affect the ratio of stock buyers and sellers, this could end up influencing stock prices, at least in the short term.

The development and application of new technologies is another factor that, in many cases, shapes the direction of stock market prices. News of companies announcing that they have reached important milestones in the development of autonomous driving vehicles, for instance, can encourage investors to buy shares of companies working on that technology if they are feeling optimistic that such technology will become widely adopted in the future. This move could affect not only the stocks of the main manufacturers but also those of their key known suppliers.

The emergence and popularization of new business models, like the ones developed by Uber (UBER) and Airbnb (ABNB), had significant effects as well, not only on the price of the stocks of these emerging companies but also on the prices of the ones perceived as their most directly affected competitors. Some of these changes may be gradual, as the new businesses consolidate, but can become more visible over time.

Other areas where the prospects for the application of new technologies —and the milestones that may be reached in their development or consolidation process— could impact stock prices, at the time of this writing, include improved wireless communications, artificial intelligence, robotics, remote health services, drone applications, genetic manipulation, and virtual reality, among others.

Companies able to quickly incorporate new technologies to effectively improve, leverage, or expand their existing operations, or the products or services they offer, as applicable to their market segment, may also be likely to attract stock buyers as well, with the subsequent effect of having their share prices gradually rise if enough investors feel optimistic about those technologies.

BUSINESS DYNAMICS

The soundness of a business and its ability to make money, as perceived by investors —usually based on the publicly available accounting, market, and other information— is a key factor to understand the price of its shares in the stock market. Some company factors that often lead to changes in the price of its stocks include the financial performance of the business, changes in its leadership and organizational structure, employee layoffs, working conditions, and mergers and acquisitions.

Financial Performance

The business performance of publicly traded companies over a given period is one of the most direct factors determining the price of their stocks in the market. Indicators such as earnings per share

(EPS) are closely monitored to assess if the quarterly earnings reports of a company meet the analysts' projections, miss the mark, or exceed those estimates. Chart 3 illustrates a scenario where a company misses and then beats the consensus estimates.

Since earnings refer to the actual profits of a firm —its net income after taxes and other costs of doing business— this is one of the most direct indications of whether a company is making money or not. If it is making money consistently, its net worth is expected to grow over time and it may be able to distribute part of the profits as dividends to its shareholders.

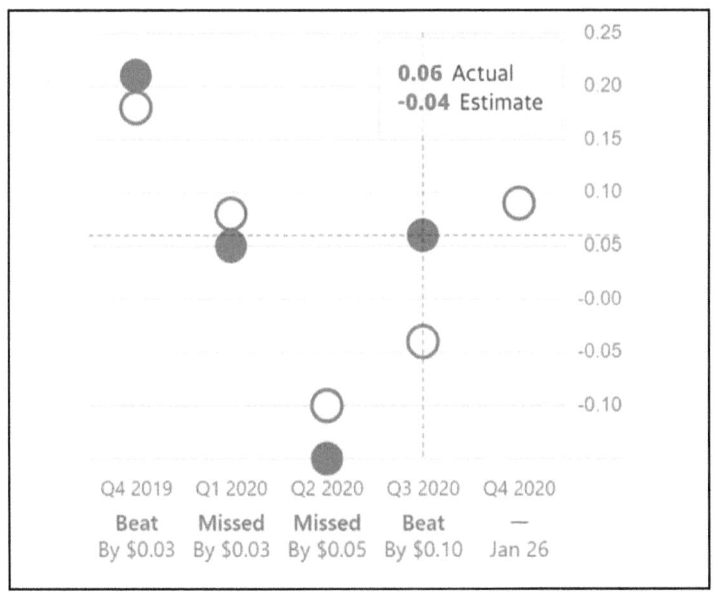

Chart 3. Earnings Per Share

EPS reports usually have an immediate effect on the price of stocks. Many investors make speculative stock and option trades in anticipation of these quarterly results, and this is often followed by after-hours trades that affect stock prices even more. However, in many cases these new prices do not last long, reverting to levels similar to the ones they had before the volatility caused by the speculations about the quarterly results, as investors look at the future prospects of the firm.

EPS is normally used in combination with the price to earnings (P/E) ratio, which indicates how much the market participants are willing to pay for each dollar of earnings. If the P/E is deemed to be moderate, some investors may consider it —along with other factors— as a candidate for purchase, but if it is considered to be high, they may decide that the stock is overvalued instead.

The market position of a firm is often analyzed in relation to its competitors. Those relationships may experience changes over time, so if investors conclude that a company is growing its market share, it can start attracting more investors and driving its stock prices up. However, this situation can happen even before companies start making profits, if there is the expectation that such businesses have good chances of being profitable in the future.

The payment of dividends is another area influencing the decision of many investors to buy, hold, or sell stocks. While companies that offer high dividend yields are attractive, since they are a source of regular income, indications that cast doubt about the ability of a firm to maintain its profitability over time, and its capacity to issue dividends, can make some investors consider alternative options. Conversely, news that a company will increase dividends is likely to attract investors.

This is particularly important because while dividends benefit shareholders, they are also an important expense for the business, a departure from resources that could have been otherwise used to improve its competitiveness and market position, purchase more modern equipment, etc.

While income stocks —those that are known for offering meaningful dividends— are typically considered in a separate category than growth stocks, which are those that normally do not offer dividends but are more likely to increase their market price over time, there are some cases of growth companies that pay dividends as well, so this does not always have to be an either/or situation.

Leadership Changes

The change of CEO in a high-visibility company usually affects the price of its stock, particularly in the case of companies whose performance is associated with the work of its leaders. Sometimes stock prices drop after these announced changes, like in situations when there is uncertainty about who the successor and their approach will be. However, in some cases stock prices increase as well, if the change in leadership is interpreted as a course correction in the right direction.

These changes can happen in the short and long term. When Steve Jobs retired from Apple (AAPL), for instance, the price of this stock initially fell more than 5 percent in the first few months, but a year later, the price of this stock had almost doubled (Olenickjun 2015).

While in practice, much of the success of a company depends on the aligned effort of senior leadership, middle management, and line workers, the conditions in which teams operate and the alignment of their efforts is in many cases attributed to the performance of the company's CEO. In part, this is because information about the internal workings of a company is not easily accessible to investors, so the track record of the CEO is something that investors can use as a reference.

Changes in the structure of an organization can also make a difference in the way investors perceive its business outlook and their interest in owning part of it. In many companies, one person takes the role of CEO and chair of the board of directors; this usually happens when the founder remains as the main shareholder and leader of the company. This gives such leaders the flexibility to shape the direction of the business and manage its communications with great leeway, creating situations where the company performance is often tied in with the success, and mistakes, of such individuals.

This consolidation of roles into one individual may also be a challenge in some cases, particularly since it limits the accountability of CEOs to their boards of directors. Likewise, while a CEO may be a visionary or a bright technical expert, they may also have some limitations in other areas. Examples include CEOs making reckless public declarations that do not put the company in its best light, facing charges for sexual harassment, making political declarations inconsistent with the values of those consuming their products or using their services, responding to public criticism in a way that antagonizes some of their key external stakeholders, etc. When so much is at stake, sometimes relying on one individual to do well in all areas could be unrealistic.

While there are examples of companies that are successful despite having different corporate arrangements, what makes sense at one time may not make as much sense at another. If complications arise, in many cases the response is to make changes to the corporate structure in a way that addresses the issue. Such movements frequently restore investors' confidence, which may lead to greater interest in acquiring part of those companies, translating into higher stock prices.

Employee Layoffs

The process of laying off staff also has implications for stock prices. While this is a highly controversial measure because of its adverse impacts on the affected workers, this is a frequent practice that, from an accounting standpoint, is seen as a way to keep costs low. In some cases, this is done to make the company profits look better, but in other cases, this action can be unavoidable if the business is not generating enough revenues to retain all its staff.

Many companies whose revenues declined during the COVID-19 pandemic, for instance, had to lay off significant numbers of employees because they had to reduce or suspend their operations, which affected their levels of profit and also caused stock price declines. Faced with this situation, their ability to reduce costs by laying off employees was, in many cases, perceived as a move that the company was not spending beyond their means when there were not enough earnings to be made. This action gave investors confidence that the company's future would not be jeopardized by overspending or increasing its debt to keep their payroll intact, encouraging them to either hold on to their stocks or buy some more at their lowered price, thus preventing further price drops.

Such moves, however, could also be detrimental for the ability of such companies to provide similar levels of service or reach the same level of quality in the future. This is particularly because of the loss of valuable human capital and people with extensive business acumen, which, in many cases, cannot be easily restored by hiring new staff when it is time to scale up operations again.

In such scenarios, the ability of a company to regain its competitive edge may depend on multiple factors, like its type of business activities, the level of specialization needed by its employees, whether its budget allowed it to retain key employees needed to transfer the company's knowledge to the new hires once recruitment resumes, and its ability to rehire furloughed workers, among others.

Working Conditions

One important area associated with working conditions in the United States is salaries. Companies known for paying low wages to their employees often face public criticism, with the subsequent discontent of many of their customers, who may be more likely to go to competitors if they consider them to be better aligned with their perceptions about the role of business in society.

Beyond that, these companies may face pressure from some of their shareholders as well, even when such companies can offer salaries that are above the minimum wages, but not enough to cover the minimum cost of living in the locations where their workers live. Data from Global Workplace Analytics (GWA) indicates that losing one valuable employee can cost employers between $10,000 and $30,000, in addition to thousands more to recruit and train new hires.

Low wages may also lead to strikes, and workers' strikes during the busiest holidays of the year, such as Black Friday, have the potential to reduce the sales of a company and its income generation prospects, which in turn will be reflected in stock prices when the quarterly EPS reports indicate that the company missed its estimates. Even before that, analysts may adjust their estimates to account for new information, which may also affect stock prices.

On the other hand, companies that take measures to ensure that their employees are well paid may also see improvements in their company revenues. Gravity Payments, for instance, is a payment processing company whose CEO decided to raise the minimum annual salary of its employees to $70,000, which led to higher employee motivation, productivity, and retention levels. Profits ended up not being affected by paying higher salaries;

in fact, they grew at twice the rate they had before this change (Keegan 2015).

The culture of a company also affects the working environment of its employees. The case of Zappos is an example that intentional efforts to promote the company's core values led to the adoption of a positive corporate culture, with important effects on employee behavior, engagement, and retention, which translated into customer satisfaction. It ultimately drove more sales and increased business performance (Cancialosi 2017), making this business attractive to investors.

As a result of the COVID-19 pandemic, the decision of many companies to allow its employees to work remotely —even after the pandemic is over— is also expected to increase the profitability of some public companies willing to adopt this approach, since it has the potential to cut office costs. With real estate being an important business expense, this move could translate into savings that can be reinvested to grow the company and/or pay dividends. According to GWA, employers can save an average of $11,000 per half-time telecommuting employee per year, and each employee could save between $2,000 and $7,000, which would add up to more than $700 billion across the United States (Denson 2019).

When dealing with overseas workers, like in the case of companies whose manufacturing or production activities are in foreign countries, there are other important aspects associated with working conditions. These include, for instance, company risks associated with workers' exposure to toxic chemicals in manufacturing plants, child labor in production processes, and forced labor among the suppliers of raw materials such as coltan and timber, among many others.

A useful resource to quickly assess labor risks in foreign countries is the app Sweat & Toil (ILAB), populated with data from the U.S. Department of Labor, which can quickly provide data on existing risks by country, economic sector, goods produced, and type of potential labor exploitation.

Even in some cases when the responsibility of ensuring adequate and safe working conditions lies not with the main company but with its primary suppliers in other countries, this could still be a cause for concern. For example, cases of alleged negligence during the firm's due diligence processes, or if corporate leaders were informed of legal violations by suppliers but failed to take corrective measures, could end up in situations that affect the company and/or its leadership.

Mergers and Acquisitions

Mergers occur when two organizations are combined to create a single organization. Their purpose is normally to seek synergies in terms of reducing costs and increasing delivery capacity, capture a greater market share, expand operations, or diversify activities, among other business benefits.

The most frequent scenario of companies coming together, however, is when one company acquires another, even when such a move is called a merger. The acquiring company may integrate the business operations of the other one into its own processes and/or brand, or continue operating the business as a separate entity but seeking synergies between both companies, which can be done gradually.

If both participating companies are publicly traded, the prices of their stocks usually experience changes, at least in the short term. This usually happens from the moment the news about the potential acquisition talks are known, long before the actual acquisition takes place.

Stock price changes in these cases are experienced differently, according to the role of each company. The shares of the company being acquired tend to increase in price, especially because of the synergies and management support expected from the buying company, the validation of the business potential implicitly recognized by the acquiring company, and also because the buying company usually buys the shares of the firm being acquired above their market price, as an incentive for the sale.

Conversely, the stock price of the acquiring company normally tends to decrease, particularly because acquisitions often represent a significant expense —the profitability of which is sometimes not readily apparent for investors— besides the above-market cost of the purchase that is usually involved. Another reason is that, in many cases, those purchases increase the company's debt, with interest that needs to be paid for that borrowed money, which reduces the profitability of the acquisition.

In some cases, however, the companies involved in merger and acquisition talks do not reach agreements, or the proposed transactions are challenged by regulators, so the expected deal may not go through. When that happens, it can reverse the direction of the stock price changes.

POLICIES AND POLITICS

The price of securities in the stock market can be affected by regulatory processes, legal proceedings, political influence, policies prioritizing certain sectors, and actions targeting specific companies, among other related factors. These are explained in greater detail below.

Regulatory Actions

Fines on companies can be imposed for different reasons, and by both national regulators and foreign governments. For instance, when an electronic device maker with global sales gets fined in a European country over water resistance claims, this event increases the likelihood that other jurisdictions could also impose fines on the company for similar reasons.

Antitrust actions, which are intended to protect trade from monopolies and unfair business practices, could also affect the business competitiveness of companies, and their stock prices. These could include, for instance, actions by the Federal Trade Commission (FTC), recommendations issued by the House or Senate antitrust committees, Department of Justice lawsuits, European Union actions, etc.

An example of such actions is the one initiated in 2020 by the FTC and the attorneys general of several states against Facebook (FB), based on alleged anticompetitive behavior intended to put rivals out of business, centered on its market dominance brought by the acquisition of other platforms like Instagram and WhatsApp (Swartz 2020). Other antitrust actions include the ones against Google by the Justice Department, and against Amazon and Apple by the European Union.

Such proceedings are usually lengthy, with costly legal fees, and in some cases may end up in fines, enhanced government oversight, restrictions on future expansion plans, or modifications of the corporate structures of the involved entities. However, they may also end up in situations without substantial changes to the existing operations of these companies, particularly in cases of already consolidated activities that were previously approved by government agencies.

In the case of Chinese firm Alibaba (BABA), in 2020 its stock prices declined as a result of a fine imposed by China's State Administration for Market Regulation, as well as an antitrust probe launched by this agency into its business practices. Similarly, the anticipated IPO of Ant Group, an affiliate company of Alibaba, was withdrawn because of concerns by the China Securities Regulatory Commission.

Each of these scenarios can be interpreted in different ways by investors. If many of them react to such news by selling their stocks, this causes their prices to drop, at least in the short term. They may also hold on to their positions until there is greater clarity on the process, or dismiss some of these processes as not meaningful in relation to the expected business prospects of the company.

Class actions also affect stock market prices. A study published in the *Journal of Business & Securities Law* indicates that these events show statistically significant negative abnormal returns, particularly at the time of their filing and its preceding weeks, with firms in the non-service sector and financial firms — especially for claims related to 10(b) securities fraud— being the ones that experience greater adverse impacts (Klock 2016).

Lawsuits and other legal claims, including those filed by consumers and other organizations, also have the potential to affect stock prices. In the case of Apple, the price of its shares increased when it won a patent infringement lawsuit against Samsung. Yet Apple was also the subject of a lawsuit by Epic Games, and if the plaintiff were to be successful, it could decrease the level of commissions Apple receives, not only from Epic Games but from other app developers as well, since they could use such a ruling as a precedent to demand similar treatment (Nickelsburg 2019). Since app commissions are an important source of profits, this ruling could affect its stock prices.

The end of certain trading restrictions can also affect stock prices. Companies that issue initial public offerings (IPOs), for instance, in many cases see the price of their stocks drop, at least temporarily, after their lock-up periods end. These periods typically last between three and six months, during which company insiders and some early investors cannot sell their stocks. If investors who were waiting for these restrictions to lift sell large numbers of shares at that time, this can create a greater number of sellers than buyers, driving stock prices down.

Political Influence

Presidential cycles also affect stock prices. When a new president is elected, their policies are likely to favor some sectors over others, and companies in the favored sectors are more likely to see the price of their shares increase, or for those likely to face greater scrutiny, decrease. Key areas likely to be affected are taxes, government spending, interest rates, and trade.

An administration concerned about climate change, for instance, can open more opportunities for renewable energy companies and issue additional restrictions and/or raise taxes for those involved in fossil fuel production. Canada, for example, established that as part of the government's economic response to COVID-19, large businesses that apply for government loans will need to start publishing climate disclosure reports and other environmental sustainability data (Degnarain 2020).

From a historical perspective, according to Yardeni Research, the U.S. stock market performed better (approximately 4 percent on average) when there was a divided government, that is, when the political party of the elected president did not control both chambers of Congress (Smith 2020).

Political influence is also an important driver of stock prices. When Microsoft (MSFT) was awarded a $10 billion contract to provide cloud computing services to the Pentagon, its company stocks surged 3 percent, while at the same time the shares of Amazon, which was also competing for this contract, experienced a decline of 0.92 percent when it was announced that it had not won (Stewart 2019).

However, Amazon then filed a court claim to prevent Microsoft from starting to work on this contract, arguing that the sitting president's bias against Amazon harmed its chances of winning this contract.

Amazon's stock prices also decreased following the protests and public criticism that happened in the weeks before it announced the cancelation of its plans to build a second headquarters in Long Island City, New York. In a statement, the company said that "*a number of state and local politicians have made it clear that they oppose our presence and will not work with us to build the type of relationships that are required to go forward with the project*" (Fiegerman 2019).

Similarly, a private company such as ByteDance, the Chinese-based parent company of the social media app TikTok, had plans to go public and raise substantial amounts of money to expand its business activities, with a valuation of about $50 billion. However, this company faced challenges in the United States over political concerns about the potential use by the Chinese government of the information collected from the app's users (Deter 2020). Political pressure forced a partnership proposal with Oracle (ORCL), which was ultimately not accepted, disrupting the company's plans to go public.

This happened in the middle of a trade war between the United States and China that imposed tariffs on imports valued at hundreds of billions of dollars. A study on the effects of this trade war, conducted in a sample of close to three thousand firms, found that U.S. and Chinese tariff announcements caused U.S. companies to lose at least 6 percent of their equity value —approximately $1.7 trillion (Anderson 2020).

Stimulus packages during recessionary periods also affect stock prices, particularly because they can reassure investors that such measures may provide an important push for the economy to recover, along with broader measures like the reduction in interest rates. The discussions, deals, or failure to reach agreements on such stimulus packages, however, often become a source of stock price volatility.

When a company has operations in foreign countries, there are additional influential factors that can affect not only stock prices but the viability of their operations in those countries as well. These include political instability, economic crises, social unrest, and even the potential nationalization of a company's assets and operations in the country, among other risks.

There are also many politically and socially significant events that affect the United States in considerable ways but that do not end up causing changes in stock market prices. One of the reasons is that investors assess the likely impact of such incidents in the future, and they may deem some of those events as short-lived or not relevant to the ability of companies to continue being profitable.

SOCIAL FACTORS

The Internet is full of information about the stock market, individual stocks, and the companies and products behind those stocks. This information includes analyses, reflections, opinions, commentaries, advertorials, and explicit or implicit recommendations. These may be disseminated via news articles, blog posts, social media posts, newsletters, etc. A simple web search provides plenty of information casting companies and their shares in a positive or negative light, which sometimes affects the perceptions of investors regarding such securities.

There are also TV programs with guest speakers that discuss their analyses of stocks, disclosing the ones they already own and the ones they intend to purchase, and even when they may not issue explicit recommendations, they often provide a sense of social validation for viewers about certain stocks, or have the potential to convey an idea about their likely stock market performance.

While these pieces of information are not by themselves drivers of stock price changes, because for the most part their influence is minimal in comparison with the size of the market, and because of the diversity of market participants and their preferred information channels, there may be certain circumstances where they can become more influential. If the source is credible enough and the message is broadly disseminated, certain messages may be able to induce fear among investors and convince them to sell their stocks or buy new ones, and if this were to happen massively, it could cause significant price fluctuations.

The following example illustrates this situation. In February 2018, when a reality TV star commented that she was no longer using the social media app Snapchat (SNAP), the recent redesign of which had left many users frustrated, the price of this stock fell by 6 percent (Yurieff 2018). While the downtrend continued in the next months, a year and a half later it had recovered to levels similar to the ones it had before this comment, and even tripled by the end of 2020. While that comment was not the cause of the decline in itself, since the underlying condition was consumers' preferences and their dissatisfaction with that particular product update, the public comment of this influencer seems to have acted as the straw that broke the camel's back —the catalyst that led investors to believe that this product was poised to lose its market share to competitors.

Elon Musk's tweets, which are followed by more than forty-seven million users, also have been portrayed as influential in stock prices. They have been associated with significant short-term changes in the stock price of companies such as GameStop, Etsy, Signal, and Tesla.

The emergence of specialized online forums with large numbers of retail investors can also make a significant difference in the short-term variability of stock prices. If they decide to buy a certain stock together, the price of such stocks could skyrocket and produce short squeezes, which are characterized by rapid stock price rises that put pressure on those traders who shorted the stock. In January 2021, the major news outlets reported a trend that started when the Reddit group r/wallstreetbets —which has more than nine million members— organized a campaign to buy GameStop (GME) together. As a result, the price of this stock increased by more than 1,200 percent in a little over a week. As Fung (2021) explained, this type of collective trading activity could make stocks lift or sink, exposing the short-term market manipulation effect that large trading volumes can have on stock prices. This is something that institutional investors such as large hedge funds have been able to do on a routine basis, and that online groups of retail investors have now started to do in a more coordinated manner as well.

Beyond social media, the social context in which a company operates also makes a difference in the process. A company whose business is building roads in foreign countries, for instance, may face issues like corruption during the bidding processes, lawsuits over the terms of the contracts, social conflicts such as worker strikes that force operations to stop, acts of vandalism during riots, and delays in the land acquisition processes that lead to substantial cost overruns, among many others. News of such setbacks released on mainstream media could affect the price of company stocks if the issue is not just localized but has the potential to disrupt the whole company.

Boycott campaigns organized around the products or services of a company represent another area with the potential to affect the price of a company's shares and harm its reputation. A study published in the *Journal of Consumer Policy* found that "*consumer boycott announcements were followed by statistically significant decreases in stock prices for the target firms*" (Pruitt and Friedman 1986). The analysis of more recent boycott campaigns, however, indicates that, in many cases, opponents and advocates usually cancel each other out, and that the setbacks caused by boycotts are often short-lived and for the most part do not affect company profits, even though they may affect a firm's reputation (Blanton 2018; Bond 2019).

While all these factors could be influential on the price of stocks at a given moment, it is important to recognize that many of the factors leading to the short-term variability of stock prices may not end up affecting their long-term prospects. The long-term price of stocks is fundamentally associated with the ability of a company to produce profits as a result of its business operations, and to maintain or improve its position in the market over the long run. Supply and demand determine when there are more buyers than sellers, and vice versa, which is ultimately the reason why stock prices change, depending on the aggregated decisions of investors at a given time.

3

ANALYZING STOCK PERFORMANCE

How do investors make sense of the abundance of factors that could affect stock prices? In an ideal scenario, decisions to buy and sell stocks could benefit from the advice of a multidisciplinary team of economists, accountants, finance specialists, business managers, socio-political scientists, and subject-matter experts, among others. In practice, however, investors must often make decisions by themselves, but helped by a variety of resources that can assist them in this process.

There are different methods to analyze stocks and securities, but the two main ones are fundamental analysis and technical analysis. Some investors choose a combination of both, or develop modified versions with additional elements of their preference. These are explained next.

FUNDAMENTAL ANALYSIS

Fundamental analysis is a method that seeks to discover the intrinsic value of stocks and other securities to assess whether their market price is overvalued or undervalued, in relation to the value of the underlying company, providing investors with a means to make informed decisions.

The intrinsic value of stocks can be inferred from the analysis of the financial aspects of the issuing companies, such as cash flow, income, assets, and liabilities. This information provides a detailed view of the past commercial performance of a firm, which allows analysts to extrapolate those values and estimate its future financial performance as well.

Important information about a company can be extracted from income statements, balance sheets, profit margins, and growth estimates, among others. These figures can be readily accessed for free in the Financials, Statistics, and Analysis tabs of Yahoo Finance®, for instance, or through similar websites that provide specialized information about companies listed in stock exchanges.

Accounting metrics and financial analyses can then be assessed together with macroeconomic factors such as interest rates, inflation rates, unemployment, and gross domestic product growth. Microeconomic factors like earnings per share (EPS), price to earnings (P/E) ratio, debt-to-equity ratio, book value, and dividend yields also play an important role in this type of analysis, within the context of the supply and demand associated with the products or services provided by a company.

The intrinsic value of a company is then compared to its market capitalization, also known as the market value of equity. This is calculated by multiplying the current market price of the stock by the total number of outstanding shares, which can be found in a company's balance sheets.

The quantitative financial analysis is also complemented with the qualitative analysis of the economic conditions shaping market trends, such as the political environment, regulatory actions, market competition, management structure, and customers' perceptions about a firm. These analyses can be carried out either from a bottom-up or top-down approach.

Investors analyze the meaning of the quantitative figures in the context of the business and its position in the market. For instance, businesses are expected to make money, and EPS can provide a good idea of how well a company is meeting its expected net profits every quarter. However, there may also be cases of companies with future growth potential but that are not profitable yet.

Likewise, a company's level of debt should be assessed together with its intended use. While debt increases the level of risk of a company, companies with high levels of debt that use it to increase their capacity to produce more goods or services with strong market demand are regarded differently than the ones that use debt to cover expenses arising from inefficient business models.

The overall assumption is that fundamental analysis can help investors identify companies with promising growth development priced below their intrinsic value, which would lead to higher stock prices once others realize it, while also helping investors determine when stocks are overpriced.

Assessing the intrinsic value of stocks, however, is not a straightforward process. As Maverick pointed out, there is a considerable degree of difficulty in such estimations, particularly when it comes to intangible assets, accuracy of information, and choice of methodology (like discounted cash flow or liquidation value), among other factors, which can lead to significant levels of variation across different analysts' estimations of intrinsic value (2020).

Even if the fundamental aspects of a business are not examined comprehensively, the core aspects of a business, reflected in indicators such as earnings per share, debt, and P/E ratio, can provide relevant insights into a company's valuation in relation to its stock market price, which can be important in the analysis of stocks prior to conducting market transactions.

Readers interested in learning more about fundamental analysis may want to consider books like *The Essays of Warren Buffett: Lessons for Corporate America* by Warren Buffett and Lawrence Cunningham (2015), *Learn to Earn: A Beginner's Guide to the Basics of Investing and Business* by Peter Lynch and John Rothchild (1996), and *The Intelligent Investor* by Benjamin Graham (1986). The book *Fundamental Analysis for Dummies* by Matthew Krantz (2016) also provides a simplified introduction.

TECHNICAL ANALYSIS

Technical analysis seeks to understand the behavior of the markets, and the ones of its buyers and sellers, based on the assumption that "*prices move in trends and trends tend to continue until something happens to change the supply-demand balance*" (Edwards and McGee 2010).

Through the analysis of financial charts, technical analysis helps technicians and investors identify probable trends in the stock market to guide their recommendations or investment decisions.

Technical analysis relies on the identification of visual patterns and trading volumes, connecting past data points to determine and forecast future trend developments. It can be applied to estimate the price trends of stocks, commodities, futures, and other securities.

Charles Dow, a co-founder of the Dow Jones Company and the *Wall Street Journal*, outlined an investment theory based on the idea that the price of stocks reflects the overall trends of the economy, and that these trends can be modeled and charted to inform investor's decisions. These include primary trends, such as the ones of a bull or a bear market; sideways trends; and trend reversals. There are also secondary trends, which can go against the primary trends, explaining in part the volatility of stock prices. Another premise is that markets are efficient, which assumes that stock prices in the market incorporate all publicly available information, including expectations for future trends and events, and that all market participants can have access to the same information (Rhea 1932). These assumptions, placed in the context of the law of supply and demand, provide a foundation for technical analysis, helping investors understand how the stock market behaves.

Trends can be classified according to their time frame. These can include day trends, short-term trends, medium-term trends, long-term trends, and secular trends. To understand the conditions associated with trend changes, the analysis of trends is supported by the use of stock charts.

There are many different kinds of stock charts. One of the most basic ones is line charts, which show the closing prices of stocks over a given period, allowing the identification of trends over time. Solid candlestick charts offer additional information, such as the stock prices at the opening and closing moments of the specified interval, making it a popular choice for investors. In colored charts, solid green candles indicate that the closing price is higher than the opening price of the specified interval, and if the solid candles are red, the closing prices are lower than the opening ones. The wicks at the top and bottom of each candle indicate the highest and lowest prices reached within the specified interval, respectively. There are also hollow candlesticks, which are read differently than solid candlesticks, as well as bar charts, among many others.

Intervals on a chart can be personalized according to user preferences. On a chart with a date range of five years, for instance, each interval could be a week, a month, or a year long. On a chart displaying one day of price data, each interval could be set to minutes or hours. A common approach is to look at larger time frames first before focusing on the narrower ones.

Stock market trends can be spotted by connecting successive price points. For instance, the use of the moving average (MA) indicator, calculated based on the closing prices of a number of preceding periods, can help investors visualize the trends by smoothing out price fluctuations.

To facilitate the visual analysis of trends, investors can plot both short-term and medium-term MA lines on the same chart. For instance, they can compare the 200-day MA with the 50-day MA, and these lines can form patterns that can be analyzed to understand market trends.

Investors can also use channel lines, which are successive high lines and low lines near the upper and lower limits of the price fluctuations, based on a given number of preceding periods, plotted automatically by charting software. In Yahoo Finance, once users type in and search for a company by name or ticker, the summary data has the option to expand the stock chart in full-screen mode. Once that option is clicked, users can add indicators such as zigzag, moving averages, Bollinger bands, etc.

Support and Resistance

Two important concepts in technical analysis are support and resistance. The support line represents the bottom line of a price range. It is a reference line from which the downtrend can start reversing, or continue if prices were to go further down than in the preceding periods. The resistance line represents the top level of a price range and follows the same logic as the support line. These lines are illustrated in Chart 4.

Support and resistance lines can be plotted on charts, and their placement can be calculated using indicators like pivot points, Fibonacci retracement levels, Bollinger bands, and Donchian channels. MA and trend lines can also be helpful to assess support and resistance levels.

Resistance and support create the zone within which most price movements are expected to happen, helping investors identify potential trend reversals, unless stock prices break through those lines, in which case the bandwidth may expand to reflect the latest price changes.

Rather than fixed lines, support and resistance can be seen as flexible zones, allowing for false breaks — situations where prices can go past those lines without being considered as breakthroughs— being mindful of the fact that past behavior does not predict future events, so these lines can be a starting point in the analysis, along with other price-change drivers.

Another helpful tool to assess support and resistance is the stochastic oscillator, which compares the current price of a stock in relation to its price range over a period of time, indicating if a stock is oversold or overbought. Since oscillator values are range-bound, they will fall between 0 and 100. For instance, a value of over 80 would mean that the stock is overbought, and if the value goes below 20 it would suggest that the stock is oversold.

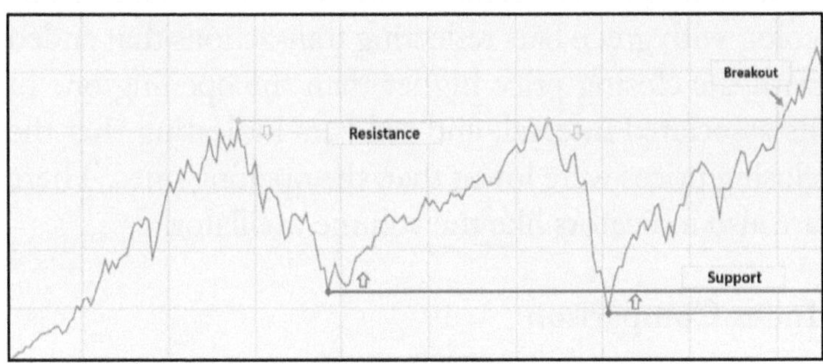

Chart 4. Support and Resistance Levels

Many traders use the upper and lower ranges of the stochastic oscillator to identify potential entry points for trades, in many cases interpreting overbought stocks as a selling signal and considering oversold stocks as a buying opportunity. This oscillator can be used together with other indicators, like the relative strength index (RSI) and the moving average convergence divergence (MACD).

Trade Volume

Another key factor in technical analysis is volume confirmation. Once trendline patterns are identified, their strength needs to be confirmed by the volume of transactions. For instance, if the price of a stock has been decreasing until it reaches a given support level, and then starts a clear upward trend confirmed by hundreds of millions of transactions, then volume acts as a confirmation of that trend reversal, at least in the short term, until new events happen.

Volume bars can usually be seen or enabled in the bottom area of stock charts and can be differentiated by color, with green bars reflecting transactions that ended with the closing price higher than the opening one of its associated interval, and red bars indicating that the closing prices were lower than the opening ones. There are also indicators like the volume oscillator.

Index Comparison

Another important element in trend analysis is the comparison of specific stocks against their sector and the stock market in general. This is because individual stocks often trend in the same direction as the market. For instance, an investor interested in a biotechnology company who is looking at stock trends could benefit from also looking at the performance of the Nasdaq Biotech Index, as well as the major indexes such as the Nasdaq 100 and the S&P 500.

The analysis of trends in international stock markets —such as the Nikkei 225 in Japan, the FTSE 100 in England, and the DAX in Germany—can also inform the analysis of domestic trends affecting stocks and indexes, particularly in the opening sessions in the U.S. stock market.

The futures contracts on stock indexes can also provide important insights into price trends. For instance, investors can look at the percentage of change in the S&P 500 E-Mini and the Dow Futures Mini, which can help them understand the price gaps between the closing prices of a session and the opening prices at the next day's trading session. Looking at the latest news about the potential causes of price variations can also help investors in their analysis of trends.

While investor psychology is a broader subject and offers additional elements that can influence price variation, the CBOE Volatility Index (VIX) can be a helpful indicator of the attitudes of investors toward the stock market; it's commonly known as an indicator of the level of market fear.

The identification of specific chart patterns used to predict future trends is outside the scope of this book, but investors interested in developing the skills to read charts can consult other specialized resources and see how technical analysis can assist them in their investment decisions.

To learn more about technical analysis, readers may want to consider books such as *Getting Started in Technical Analysis* by Jack Schwager (1999), *Technical Analysis of the Financial Markets* by John Murphy (1999), *Charting and Technical Analysis* by Fred McAllen (2012), and *Technical Analysis Explained* by Martin Pring (2014). *Technical Analysis for Dummies* by Barbara Rockefeller (2020) provides a basic introduction, while those interested in taking it even further can review the preparation materials for the Chartered Market Technician (CMT) exams.

OTHER METHODOLOGIES

This section includes brief mentions of additional ways to approach stock analysis, such as stock-picking methodologies that combine aspects of both fundamental and technical analysis to facilitate their application, while also considering environmental, social, and governance aspects.

Stock Picking Methodologies

There are many methodologies intended to increase the odds of investors picking stocks with the greatest chances of success, many of which combine elements of fundamental and technical analysis. As John Cunnison, vice president and chief investment officer at Baker Boyer Bank, pointed out, a strong analysis of companies must consider "*both qualitative factors (company culture, employee and customer satisfaction, brand recognition and loyalty) and quantitative factors (revenue growth, profitability, cash flow, debt levels)*" (Likos 2020).

One methodology that puts different factors together is the CAN SLIM approach, developed by William O'Neil (2009), founder of the *Investor's Business Daily*, which focuses on aspects such as the analysis of earnings, products, and relationship with the market in a structured way.

Investors following a method based on Wyckoff's market cycle, which is explained in Chart 2, usually start by determining the current market trend, assessing the strength of a given security and its relationship with the broader stock market trend, considering if the potential rewards are worth the risks, and determining the best time to buy those securities (Binance 2020).

Another approach, developed by Lex van Dam (2012), former head of equities trading at Goldman Sachs, is to use a checklist and scorecards. If looking at a company in a given industry, investors can develop lists of relevant criteria. Each of those items is then assigned values, which produce a total score that can be compared with other companies to help investors make more informed decisions.

Turner and Scott (2013) also developed a method that combines the analysis of stock charts with company fundamentals, which enables investors to create customized lists that can be refined using techniques that balance the desire to maximize returns with risk management aspects.

Filtering companies that meet certain criteria is another approach, which can be achieved with the help of stock screeners. As Greenblatt explains, this can help investors identify companies by market capitalization, returns on assets, company types, and analyst recommendations, among other criteria (2010).

MapSignals uses a different approach, based on algorithms to find stocks that institutional investors are buying —and verifying that the company fundamentals are solid. These institutions' large purchases tend to drive stock prices up, letting investors benefit from those moves (Bodner and Downey 2020).

Other investors instead look at the stocks of low-growth companies in sectors that pay significant dividends, such as utilities, consumer staples, and REITs, which can provide a source of regular income; those dividends can be reinvested to increase investors' stakes in those companies.

Stocks of companies in emerging markets can also be part of a portfolio allocation strategy. In such cases, the geographical location of such firms can be an important criterion, considering regional trends as well, which can be used in combination with other fundamental or technical criteria.

Other investors prefer to turn to indexes instead, which offer broad diversification of stocks (Bogle 2017). These could include broad market indexes or sector-specific ones. With this approach, there is no need to select individual stocks; rather, investors just define the characteristic of the index and the most appropriate investment instrument, such as low-cost mutual funds or index-tracking ETFs.

Environmental, Social, and Governance (ESG) Factors

In this approach, the way of selecting stocks is based on the combination of traditional methods with the analysis of the ESG factors related to a company, and its associated ESG ratings.

This approach focuses on the sustainability aspects of a company or fund, recognizing it as a crucial aspect of long-term success, and acknowledging the risks of potential unintended outcomes if an organization were to fail to take ESG into account.

This is particularly relevant in light of several studies that indicate ESG strategies have proven that they can beat the market (Collinson 2020; Stevens 2019; Derousseau 2018; RBC 2012).

Socially responsible investing, of which ESG is a specific version, is attractive to investors not only in terms of the business prospects of a company, but also for employees seeking to work for a company aligned with their values —increasing motivation levels and reducing cognitive dissonance— and for the communities that host or are shaped by the presence of a company.

The factors considered when evaluating the ESG strength of a company or investment include:

- **Environmental**: This includes company actions surrounding issues such as pollution (e.g., oil spills, release of toxic chemicals, greenhouse gas emissions), environmentally friendly products, organic components, land use and contribution to land conversion, waste generation and disposal, and the exclusion of activities like fossil fuel extraction, animal testing, nuclear energy, palm oil and tobacco growing, and genetically modified organisms, among others.

- **Social**: This includes aspects like labor conditions of employees and supply chain workers, diversity in the workplace, retention/promotion efforts, community outreach and support, gender aspects, occupational and community health and safety, and the exclusion of activities like gambling, controversial weapons, alcohol, and adult entertainment. Criticism about the use of conflict minerals by a company, for instance, illustrates the importance of the supply chain.

- **Governance**: This includes aspects like the composition of boards of directors, the presence of potential conflicts of interest in top corporate roles, transparency about corporate policies, the application of codes of ethics, grievance redress mechanisms, anti-corruption provisions, reporting arrangements, norms-based screening, auditing systems, independent certifications, and cybersecurity risk management procedures, among others.

The labor conditions of employees, and the workers of suppliers, are an important part of ESG. The reputational risks associated with companies engaged in child or forced labor as part of their production processes or acquisition of raw materials, for instance, which are prevalent in industries like agriculture, garment making, and mining, could cause significant damage to a company when it becomes known that its local suppliers engage in those types of practices.

If a company's executives know of potential human rights violations in their supply chains and choose to cover them up, fail to take steps to investigate the claims, or avoid taking corrective actions based on the findings of such investigations, this could be detrimental for a company. This type of inactivity may lead to negative press, company boycotts, the firing of top executives, lawsuits, or fines, among many other potential adverse effects that could affect the reputation of a company.

The good standing that comes with maintaining socially and environmentally responsible policies, along with clear governance setups, can help companies thrive over time, obtain tax benefits in some cases, and experience profitable financial returns in the long run.

Competitors that fall behind in upholding the ESG factors that are increasingly important to investors, the government, and society risk facing a context characterized by a growing gap between the values of those stakeholders and the business practices of such companies, which could encourage consumers and investors to look for alternative firms with better ESG records.

There are many resources available to investors to learn more about which socially responsible investing options may be potentially suitable for their goals. These include The Motley Fool's overview of ESG stocks, the CFA Institute's section on ESG products, Sustainalytics' ESG research and ratings, The MSCI Principles of Sustainable Investing, Morningstar's ESG research reports, the S&P Global Indexes on ESG investments, and Responsible Investor's *ESG Magazine.*

The following websites can also help investors get started in assessing the ESG ratings and the performance of specific stocks, mutual funds, bonds, and exchange traded funds (ETFs): Yahoo Finance's Sustainable and Ethically Responsible Companies, Morningstar's ESG Screener, and dedicated websites such as deforestationfreefunds.org, genderequalityfunds.org, weaponfreefunds.org, tobaccofreefunds.org, and fossilfreefunds.org.

The different approaches to analyzing stocks discussed in this chapter can be used in combination with each other. While an investor can choose a preferred method of evaluating the future potential of a stock or security, adding elements of other approaches can provide important insights to make more informed investment decisions. For instance, an investor could use country analysis to determine the overall health of the economy in the country where a company is located or operates, as well as the country's level of risk; sector analysis to define the preferred economic sector(s) where investments can be placed; a stock-picking methodology to do a preliminary selection of which stocks to track; fundamental analysis to further determine the strength of companies whose stocks are being considered as candidates for purchase; technical analysis to assess market and stock trends; and ESG analysis to understand the sustainability of the investments under consideration.

While combining elements of different approaches is not always a straightforward process, besides the fact that many of them may require specialized knowledge, an open attitude to use all available resources may help them improve their chances of success. As Giddens pointed out, if ideas are important and illuminating, their usefulness matters more than the place where they come from (1984).

Regardless of where investors may decide to focus their analyses, and the factors they choose to consider as the most relevant in their investment decisions, carrying out a big-picture analysis in addition to reviewing the specific situation of a firm can strengthen their analyses, ensuring that the socio-economic and business context in which a company operates is taken into account.

4

DEFINING AN INVESTMENT STRATEGY

Investors who outline an investment strategy before beginning to invest in the stock market are better prepared to navigate its volatility. Such a strategy would anticipate that the market prices will go up and down, and will provide investors with a roadmap, allowing them to stay the course instead of making rash decisions as a reaction to such fluctuations.

Investing strategies normally include both entry points, with the times and/or conditions when it may be appropriate to enter the market (buy stocks), and also the circumstances and/or anticipated time frame to exit or close those positions (sell their stocks).

The right investing strategy depends on the specific circumstances and risk tolerance of each investor, which includes risk appetite and ability to take on risk. A personalized strategy can allow investors to reach their desired goals in those ways that make the most sense for them.

Investment strategies informed by risk management considerations can help investors not only grow their money but also protect their investments. Solid investment strategies need to be satisfactory not only from the point of view of the potential returns they can generate, but also in terms of the risks such approaches may involve, and include specific measures to manage those risks.

Another important investment consideration is the timing of entry and exit of the market. This is discussed in greater detail in the sections on economic trends and investor psychology, but the key message is that the timing for buying and selling can have a substantial impact on a portfolio.

In addition to the initial screening to identify potential stocks for a portfolio, which may require significant research, most strategies require some level of regular monitoring, to make adjustments as needed, rebalance a portfolio regularly, reenter trailing stop loss orders after they expire, or decide on a course of action if something significant happens to the companies whose shares investors hold that would warrant departing from a defined strategy, as applicable.

Some investing strategies —like the buy-and-hold-forever approach— require only a minimal involvement (passive investing), while others —such as swing trading— may require significantly more time doing research and trading (active investing). In many cases, some regular maintenance tasks can also be automated, like activating automatic rebalancing or setting alerts to notify investors of substantial price changes, depending on the features offered by the stockbrokers.

The time commitment needed to monitor a portfolio is also something that would need to be taken into account, so that the adopted strategy is consistent with each investor's lifestyle and availability of time. The complexity of the investment techniques to be adopted may also need to be considered, particularly since the learning curve for some approaches could be steep.

With these considerations in mind, the following sections explain different investment strategies, providing an overview of some of the main alternatives available. These are grouped according to their investment time frame, so that readers can make informed decisions when defining the strategies to manage their stock investments that best reflect their specific circumstances.

LONG-TERM INVESTING

One of the most common investment strategies is buying stocks and holding them over the long term. As Buffet pointed out in his 1996 letter to shareholders, "*Your goal as an investor should simply be to purchase, at a rational price, a part interest in an easily-understandable business whose earnings are virtually certain to be materially higher five, ten and twenty years from now*" (2016).

The focus of this strategy is on selecting the right stocks from the beginning, and then remaining invested throughout the market fluctuations, even if some periods could involve significant losses to a portfolio, like during the crisis of 2008, which took about eighteen months until the market recovered. In addition, the profits from stocks held for over a year are taxed more favorably than the ones held for a year or less.

With a long-term investing strategy, when the markets go down, investors understand that such drops are part of the market volatility and will wait for the stocks to recover, and keep growing after the dip is over, even if that recovery process takes years. The underlying idea with this approach is to avoid situations when investors buy the stocks when the market is high and sell them when the market is low, which could lead to a significant erosion of their investment capital.

To reduce the effect of market volatility in an investment portfolio, the long-term strategy is sometimes combined with an index fund investment approach. Index funds are the preferred investment vehicle of many investment experts, including Jack Bogle (2017) and Burton Malkiel (2016), particularly because their broad diversification provides a balance between the gains in the stock value of some companies and the losses of others.

An important factor to take into account when considering index funds, however, is that their broad diversification also represents a drag in the growth potential of stocks in periods when the market is rallying, in a similar way that they reduce the level of losses when the market goes down. In that sense, the proportion of index funds in an investment portfolio is to a significant extent a reflection of the risk appetite and tolerance of each specific investor.

A long-term approach to investment is sometimes paired with the dollar-cost averaging approach, which seeks to even out the differences in the purchase price of stocks caused by market fluctuations.

Cyclical investing is another approach, which seeks to take advantage of broad market cycles. For instance, when the stock market is down, investors would buy growth stocks, and when the market is up, they may start buying bonds or other defensive securities instead, holding them until the market drops, when they may focus on purchasing growth stocks again.

Another approach to investing is to replicate the portfolios of successful investors or the holdings of the best-performing ETFs. This involves identifying the assets owned by an investor or firm, determining which ones an investor feels comfortable in adding to their portfolios, and deciding upon the weight they want to assign to each of the selected securities. Lists of the best-performing ETFs in a given year can be readily accessed on the Internet, along with their top holdings. The quarterly lists of stocks owned by large institutional investors can be found in SEC records (Form 13F).

Dividends can also play an important part in a long-term investment strategy, and most stockbrokers provide a way to reinvest the dividends in the same stocks that issued them.

The advantages and soundness of the long-term investment approach are best understood by the concept of the time value of money, a core concept in corporate finance. The basic idea is that money earns interest and this interest gets compounded, which over time can add up to substantial growth if reinvested.

Gains can be improved by investing the dividends earned via dividend reinvestments (DRIPs), which also contribute to the compounded gains. Compounded earnings highlight the fact that we can not only gain interest on the original invested capital (the principal), but also on the amount gained by capital appreciation, and potentially on the reinvested dividends as well, as applicable.

Key variables to consider when assessing the future value (FV) of stocks are present value (PV), return rates (INT), and number of periods (N). With these estimated values, financial calculators and web tools can calculate the future value of stocks, whose reliability depends on how close the estimated return rates end up reflecting the actual returns of the market. While such estimates rarely hit the mark, they may provide a starting point for the analysis, along with other factors.

A common question from new investors is how long it will take them to double their money. There are free web calculators that can answer that question, and the rule of 72 may also come in handy. Investors divide 72 by the expected annual growth percentage and get the estimated number of years to double their money (Pant 2019). For instance, if the expected annual growth is 9 percent, dividing 72 by 9 results in 8, which means that it would take about eight years to duplicate their investment capital.

These calculations, however, are for reference purposes only, based on average amounts, since in practice the stock market growth is usually uneven. As Ross et al. (2019) explained, there are periods of "supernormal" growth rates, and those cannot happen indefinitely, but if we start calculating future stock prices at the wrong time, or fail to recognize nonconstant growth, this could lead to significant calculation errors and unrealistic expectations.

SWING TRADING

Swing trading refers to the practice of buying securities, like stocks and ETFs, and selling them within a few days, weeks, or months. This is a short-term investment strategy that relies on market volatility to profit from the variation in stock prices.

This strategy can be successful when a trader anticipates the correct direction that the market will move, and relies on the assumption that the trades will be profitable in most cases, which will help offset the losses that may happen when the market moves in the opposite direction.

Many swing traders rely on technical analysis, explained in a previous chapter, which refers to the analysis of patterns and trends in stock prices based on the information provided by charts.

To reduce the risk of losing a significant part of the investment capital due to market fluctuations, traders oftentimes set up stop loss orders. Once placed, these orders remain dormant until the specified condition happens, which triggers the preprogrammed selling action. Stop loss orders are explained in greater detail in chapter 9.

Sometimes the price of stocks increases substantially overnight, usually as a result of events affecting a company's operations or the market. This can happen, for instance, when, in addition to solid business prospects, the earnings per share in a quarterly earnings report are better than expected and are released outside market hours, usually after the trading session ends.

One trading technique that some apply to these situations is what Carter calls "trading the gap," which assumes that since the price of stocks in certain specific events can increase or decrease significantly in a short period, once the excitement of investors fades out, then the prices tend to return to levels closer to their original value, as a reversion to the mean (2012). While this technique is risky, traders who wish to bet on the prospects of that stock dropping its price in a few days could short the stock, or buy a put option when the price is temporarily high. Option puts are explained in greater detail in chapter 7.

These gaps can be observed when the price of stocks falls drastically in a short period as well, and swing traders could use it to their advantage. The following example illustrates this situation. In October 2017, Citron Research, a financial blog focused on short selling, released a critical report on Shopify (SHOP). The day before the report, SHOP's opening price was $114.90, and a week after the report its price had dropped to $89.35, representing a loss greater than 20 percent. A trader who bought this stock when the price reached its lows could have profited from this trade, since two months after this incident the price of SHOP had recovered to a level similar to the one before this drop, and it kept rising afterward. By December 2020, SHOP's share prices had reached levels above $1,200.

Another approach used by swing traders is based on identifying solid companies that are experiencing temporary setbacks but whose medium- and long-term prospects remain overall good. This could be done, for instance, by using stock screeners to identify and purchase stocks with low valuations in their 52-week preceding period, and then sell them once their market prices recover (Wiley 2014).

Exit points for swing traders can be defined, for instance, by placing trailing stop orders (which are explained in chapter 9), reading signals for trend reversals provided by technical analysis, watching for news that could affect the price of stocks, or by defining profit targets, which, once reached, can trigger sell actions or activate trailing stop orders that will convert into sell orders once the prices stop rising and start declining. The important aspect is for both entry and exit criteria to be clearly defined in advance.

Once the stocks or options owned by swing traders are sold, the traders move on to other trades. Consequently, to keep up with market moves and potential trend changes, this approach requires significantly more time commitment than the long-term approach to investing.

DAY TRADING

Day traders take advantage of the intraday variation in stock prices to make a profit. They see short-term market volatility as an opportunity, and normally follow a method that helps them limit their risk exposure to minimize losses. Day traders do not hold the stocks they trade overnight.

Day traders can benefit from different market scenarios if they assess the trends correctly. They can use a combination of stocks and options for their trades. They can choose to go long when they expect the prices of stocks to go up, or to go short when they expect them to go down.

Their technical denomination is pattern day traders. According to the SEC, this refers to people who buy then sell, or sell short then buy, the same security on the same day, and does that four or more times in five business days. Day traders must maintain a minimum of $25,000 on their brokerage accounts to be able to day trade, in cash and/or securities, unless sponsored by a firm conducting proprietary trading activities, in which case they are subject to different requirements.

Since stock prices do not always vary significantly within the same day, day traders able to trade larger numbers of stocks are more likely to profit even with small price changes. This is one reason, besides it being a requirement, why many day traders trade on margin, which refers to the practice of borrowing money to increase their trading capital and leverage their trading volumes.

One important skill for day traders is the analysis of charts, which can provide them with information about market trends and about movement in the stocks they trade. Charts provide different types of indicators that day traders may be able to interpret as buy or sell signals.

Because the levels of intraday price variation are unpredictable, the profit margins of a given trade can vary. That is why day traders normally keep a close watch of price trends and market news to be able to react quickly when they see signs of potential moves in the market.

Understanding investor psychology is also crucial for day traders, since the unpredictability of the market often creates situations where the market goes in the opposite direction than the one initially anticipated. Day traders must deal with the feelings of loss on a more frequent basis than long-term investors, so they must learn to identify their emotions and manage them in ways that allow them to maintain their confidence to participate in new trades even after experiencing losses.

Understanding stock market emotions is also something day traders can use to their advantage through the analysis of market sentiment indicators, through the analysis of trends in indexes like the CBOE Volatility Index (VIX), also known as a market fear gauge, which tracks the volatility expectations for the next thirty days, based on the analysis of the S&P 500 index options prices.

Having a trading method, and being disciplined about it, is important for day traders to carry out this activity in the long run. This applies, for instance, to tasks like setting up stop orders consistently and resisting the urge to keep stocks overnight to avoid selling at a loss.

OTHER INVESTMENT STRATEGIES

This section explains other investment strategies, including those where the investment decisions are based on the recommendations of investment advisors, investing via roboadvisors, algorithmic trading, and other approaches to stock market investing.

Investment Advisors

People uncomfortable with making investment decisions on their own can benefit from the personalized advice provided by licensed financial advisors or wealth managers with experience in the type of securities in which they are planning to invest. They can assist clients in building their investment plans, find stocks that fit their investment criteria, provide information about stocks they may not know about, and help them identify potential pitfalls in the process, like tax implications.

The term *financial advisor* is used more generically, while the term *investment adviser* has a specific meaning defined by the SEC, which refers to any person or firm engaged in the business of providing advice, making recommendations, issuing reports, or furnishing analyses on securities for compensation (Section 202(a)(11) of the Advisers Act).

To verify if a financial advisor is a registered provider of financial services, including both individuals and companies, visit the following link: https://brokercheck.finra.org.

An important point to consider about financial advisors is related to the way they are paid. Some of them are fee-only registered investment advisors (RIAs), which are preferable, since they have a fiduciary responsibility to act in the best interest of their clients. Other advisors receive commissions from the sale of the investments they recommend, in many cases acting mostly as salespersons whose advice may not be fully aligned with the needs of their clients.

Some financial advisors may provide advice only, and it is the investor who performs all the transactions associated with their investment activities. Financial advisors can also perform an investment management service for their clients. The funds of investors managed with the help of a financial advisor are normally held by a third party, an RIA custodian; this service is offered by some of the major stockbrokers and other specialized firms. This helps prevent the potential mismanagement of such funds due to factors like conflicts of interest.

The more knowledge investors can acquire about investing in the stock market, however, the better positioned they will be to make informed financial decisions according to their specific situation. As Lex van Dam (2012), former head of equities trading at Goldman Sachs, pointed out, "*You may have heard the old stock market saying, that when you give your money to an expert to manage, the expert ends up with your money and you end up being the expert. There is a lot of truth in that as far as I am concerned... That's why I manage my own money and that's why I think you should consider doing the same.*" Lynch and Rothchild (2000) and McAllen (2012) take a similar approach. It may be important to recognize, however, that these are experts in the field, so their perception can differ from that of some people who may prefer the personalized support advisors can provide. As Turner and Scott explained, people can still be self-directed investors even when they use financial advisors (2013).

While beginning investors can gain knowledge about the stock market on their own, with the help of specialized resources, such as this and other books and training programs, if they decide to use advisors to select stocks it is important for them to retain the responsibility to make all final investment decisions, understand the reasons for such choices, and learn the lessons that their mistakes and successes can provide.

Investing via Roboadvisors

For investors who are comfortable with technology, roboadvisors may be another avenue for investing. There used to be some limitations of this type of trading because of the risk of high trading fees associated with higher volatility in the markets, but this issue has for the most part subsided.

When using roboadvisors, investors select an investment strategy, defined according to aspects like age and level of risk tolerance, and then the company manages the investment capital of their clients following the strategy they selected. This investment service usually has annual management fees associated with it, typically a percentage of the assets under management.

In terms of performance, according to Walsh (2019), the two-year annualized returns of roboadvisors for equity investments in the period preceding June 2019 ranged between 6.49 percent and 9.2 percent, with an average of 7.24 percent. These figures underperformed the overall stock market in the same period. The performance of roboadvisors, however, is in part explained by the asset allocations selected by investors, which often includes a combination of stocks, mutual funds, and bonds. Stockbrokers often have recommended asset allocation ranges based on investors' responses to certain questions, so a lower financial return may correspond to selections that place a higher emphasis on risk management.

Some of the more innovative approaches have been also exploring the use of artificial intelligence in stock investments. Social media mentions of stocks in traders' conversations, for instance, along with market sentiment, have been used in some cases to guide automated trades, in a manner consistent with the broader investment and risk criteria defined by investors.

Algorithmic Trading

Algorithmic trading has gradually emerged as a stock market trading strategy, even though its usage is, for the most part, still limited to people with substantial knowledge of math and computer programming, particularly of languages such as Python and C#, in addition to stock trading. This type of trading is most commonly found in organizations with large volumes of trading activity, such as hedge funds and investment banks, which can afford to have such teams of traders and programmers.

For those with the right technical background and knowledge, however, the resources needed for algorithmic trading are nowadays more readily available for people interested in this activity. Platforms such as Quantopia and Quantconnect, for instance, allow traders to develop their algorithms and backtest them on historical data of the stock market for free.

Once algorithms have been developed, backtested, and adjusted until they are deemed profitable under different scenarios, they can then be exported to brokers that accept algorithmic trading, such as Interactive Brokers and Alpaca Securities. Alpaca, for instance, offers both paper trading accounts to test algorithms against live market data, and real trading accounts, which allow traders to carry out free algorithmic trading. The level of risk of this approach, however, is significantly high, given the repetitive nature of automated trades, particularly in cases of algorithms that do not include proper safeguards, omit important criteria, or are unable to recognize trend reversals.

High-frequency trading (HFT) is a subset of algorithmic trading. While algorithmic trading can in theory be applied to any trading approach, including day and swing trading, HTF focuses on placing several orders simultaneously on different markets and executing them in fractions of a second, based on predefined parameters designed to carry out such trades at a fast rate.

The investment strategies discussed in this chapter could be strengthened by taking into consideration a risk management approach, which can help investors protect their investment capital, as explained in the following chapter about managing the risks of investing.

5

MANAGING THE RISKS OF INVESTING

Managing risk is a key part of the investment process. Beginning investors must be aware of the possibility of losing the capital they invest in the stock market, as an inherent risk of investing in general, and in stocks in particular, since many of them display high levels of market volatility. Accordingly, it is paramount for new investors to understand the importance of monitoring and managing the risks to their stock portfolios, so that they can design their investment strategies with risk considerations in mind, and include proactive measures to minimize their levels of risk exposure. These aspects are explained in greater detail next.

GENERAL CONSIDERATIONS

In general terms, there is an inverse relationship between risk and reward. Lower-risk investments provide more limited gains, but they are expected to be less susceptible to the risks associated with market fluctuations. Higher risk is likely to produce greater financial gains, but there is also a higher likelihood of significant investment losses.

This relationship is a starting point in risk analysis. Under certain circumstances, however, investments with low to moderate risk may end up being riskier than initially anticipated. This is because low-risk investments are not free of risks, which can intensify, and are often assessed based on past performance, which does not guarantee future outcomes.

U.S. Treasury bills and bonds are normally regarded as low-risk investments. However, bond investors may want to consider the fact that in 2011 the U.S. credit rating was downgraded from AAA to AA+ by Standard & Poor's (BBC 2011), and that in July 2020 Fitch downgraded the United States' rating outlook to "negative" (Mashayekhi 2020). If the U.S. were to default on its commitments to pay the securities issued in the form of Treasury notes or bonds, then the risk of such investment vehicles could increase, but without any of the rewards usually associated with higher risk investments.

On the opposite side, high-risk investments do not necessarily provide greater profit opportunities than lower-risk investments. This could be the case, for instance, of companies that went public with skyrocketing prices but are unable to maintain investors' enthusiasm for long, firms whose ability to beat new competitors is uncertain, and companies that experienced big declines in their stock value and may look cheap to buy, but that may continue losing value instead or rebounding.

A similar situation may happen with new companies with innovative business models that may show promising potential, like those in the disruptive technologies field (like apps or websites in oversaturated market niches, or businesses with overoptimistic market projections). If their growth expectations or market consolidation do not happen as expected, however, investors may end up losing a significant part, or all, of the amount they invested in such securities.

One example of such a situation is Theranos, a privately held firm that was developing rapid blood tests using automated devices with innovative technologies. This firm raised funds from private investors and venture capital sources, leading to a valuation of over $10 billion. When the company failed to deliver the promised solutions, however, its value dropped substantially, until it eventually ceased operations, with significant losses for its investors (HBO 2019).

There is also an inverse relationship between investing time frame and level of risk. Depending on how conservative or aggressive a strategy is, attempts to maximize profits in short periods will normally involve investments with higher levels of risk than those investment strategies that would take longer to produce similar levels of growth.

Awareness of these scenarios is important because they help investors understand the importance of risks when investing in the stock market. A nuanced understanding of the risky aspects of the stock market can allow investors to find the optimal balance between risk and reward, according to their risk tolerance levels, and understand the dynamic nature of investment risks.

It is also important to differentiate risk from uncertainty. A practical way to look at this difference is provided by Kay and King (2020), who put forward the distinction between *resolvable uncertainty*, which can be removed or minimized by looking something up, like facts, financial metrics, or conducting probability analyses; and *radical uncertainty*, which refers to things that we do not know and whose impact cannot therefore be resolved or inferred.

There are also "black swan" events, which investors could not have anticipated until they happen but that may cause substantial or catastrophic damage. The extreme health, social, and economic impacts of the COVID-19 pandemic that the world experienced in 2020, for instance, would have been very difficult to anticipate with the information on the virus available at the end of 2019.

Being aware of radical uncertainty as an inherent risk that could affect stock prices can help investors have a broader view of the context in which the market operates, and introduce an element of caution when planning and executing their trades. The advice of James Glassman (2020), author of the book *Safety Net: The Strategy for De-Risking Your Investments in a Time of Turbulence*, is that investors could benefit from taking a chance on the unknown, and that in this context it helps to be a long-term investor, buy stocks that pay dividends, and consider companies with great ideas.

RISK MANAGEMENT METHODOLOGY

The focus of a risk management approach, as it applies to stock market participants, is to protect their investment capital. This can be facilitated by the systematic practice of identifying the factors that could affect the chances of reaching the intended profit targets, assessing their probability of occurrence and their likely severity if they happen, and defining preventive and corrective actions to minimize their adverse effects on a portfolio.

While there are many approaches to risk management in the stock market, the identification and assessment of risks can benefit when an investor carries out the following general activities: developing a list of the main events, processes, or decisions that could potentially lead to adverse effects on an investor's portfolio; conducting an analysis and determination of whether the socio-political and economic context in which business operations take place may increase the likelihood and/or intensity of risks; and assessing if the relevant company has the capacity and the means to apply appropriate measures to manage the risks identified if they were to materialize or intensify, as applicable, and determine if that situation increases their level of exposure and/or vulnerability.

These considerations can help determine the level of risk of each of the entries in the risk list, or rows in a table, and rank them using categories such as low, medium, and high. A more nuanced approach, however, which can enable investors to further fine-tune the levels of risk, can be achieved by using categories such as low, moderate, substantial, and high (WB 2014).

Activities that an investor may decide to place in the low-risk category, for instance, include having their money in interest-bearing bank accounts, such as savings accounts and certificates of deposit, or investing in government-backed securities like Treasury bills and government bonds.

Examples of investments in the moderate category could include index funds, diversified mutual funds with low or no fees, diversified ETFs, and investment-grade corporate bonds, which are usually those with AAA to BBB ratings, depending on the levels used by the credit rating agency.

The substantial risk category could include, for instance, investments in large capitalization stocks traded in the major stock exchanges, like the NYSE and Nasdaq, and the purchase of long-term deep-in-the-money option calls as a stock replacement strategy, provided that the percentage to break even is low —something in the neighborhood of 2 percent or less.

The high-risk category could then be used for trades that involve higher levels of speculation, such as non-investment-grade bonds, also known as junk bonds, which present a higher risk of default; penny stocks (those trading for 5$ or less); over-the-counter (OTC) transactions (which refer to trading activity outside the major stock exchanges like the NYSE and Nasdaq); selling put options, naked calls, and trading short-term out-of-the-money options (discussed in chapter 7); algorithmic trading; and purchasing emerging markets stocks, particularly those from companies in countries with high levels of uncertainty, among others.

It is important to notice, however, that the assignment of risk levels can vary significantly across investors, depending on factors such as their risk tolerance, level of knowledge and experience investing in the stock market, investing horizon, professional background, familiarity with the business processes and the market conditions in which a business operates, and knowledge of the country dynamics where the companies under consideration are located, among many other factors.

The focus of risk management measures is normally on the entries with high and substantial risks, regarding which it is helpful to identify contingency measures proportionate to their level of risk. For low and moderate entries, the measure on those cases could be in most cases limited to monitoring, unless new information comes to light that may warrant risk classification changes.

Also important in the process of defining risk-management measures is the recognition of the areas where investors have control or influence, via activities such as setting risk tolerance levels, aligning trading actions with investment plans, and using practical measures like stop loss orders.

Having a risk management strategy in place can help investors assess the risk to their prospective investments, and think in advance of potential actions in response to adverse scenarios.

PRACTICAL ACTIONS

Being such a crucial aspect of the long-term resilience of a portfolio, risk management measures inclusion should be at the core of every stock market investment strategy. Here are some practical actions that investors can consider when preparing their investment strategies.

- **Avoiding risky transactions.** Learning to recognize and avoid high-risk investments can make a big difference in the health of a portfolio. Staying away from shares of struggling companies, junk bonds, and penny stocks, and avoiding the selling of naked calls and unprotected puts, among others, can provide an initial filter before applying other risk-mitigation measures.

- **Diverse asset allocation.** An asset allocation informed by risk management considerations contributes to the development of a more resilient investment strategy. A portfolio with a combination of stocks, ETFs, index funds, bonds, and commodities —either as direct investments or as the underlying securities of derivative instruments, like options and futures— will be more resilient than a portfolio composed only of stocks.

- **Portfolio diversification.** Broad diversification of investments across different sectors of the economy is also important in terms of risk management. The more independent the different types of securities selected are from one another, the better placed those investments would be to withstand market fluctuations. Variety in the types of stocks can add resilience to a portfolio as well, including combinations of growth, value, and defensive stocks, and shares of companies in different countries and with different market capitalizations. Such distribution can be weighted and adjusted according to the investors' risk management analyses.

- **Dollar cost averaging.** When it comes to stock purchases, making regular purchases of stocks — and dividend reinvestments, if applicable— may help offset the highs and lows of the stock market purchase prices over time. This is particularly relevant for long-term investors whose funds regularly increase, like employees who invest part of their monthly salaries in the stock market.

- **Index investing.** Index funds are one way to gain partial ownership of all the different companies contained in a given index, such as the S&P 500 or the Nasdaq 100, which could spread the risk and smooth out the short-term variation in the price of individual stocks, without sacrificing potential long-term growth. The S&P 500 index is often regarded as including the stocks of some of the most solid companies in the market (Boggle 2017).

- **Bond strategy.** Since stocks and bonds often show an inverse relationship, a bond strategy may be also helpful to manage risk. When optimism about the stock market prevails, there may be more investors selling bonds to buy stocks, and fewer buyers for bonds, whose value may drop as stock prices go up. However, there are also situations when stocks and bonds move in the same direction, since bond prices are primarily affected by interest rates, which have a strong inverse relationship with bonds (Tillier 2016). Accordingly, bond prices are more likely to be lower when both interest rates and stock prices are high, and those bonds can help protect the value of a portfolio when the price of stocks goes down.

- **Position sizing.** Defining money management parameters can also help spread the investment capital across different securities. This may involve, for instance, ensuring that the money available to invest at a given time is divided into several trades, and that each of those trades does not exceed a certain percentage of the total purchasing power. As Van Tharp pointed out, position sizing can make a significant difference in the long-term value of a portfolio (2006), particularly since trading fees are no longer an incentive to minimize the number of transactions.

- **Protective puts.** Buying put options can be used as a hedging strategy to protect the value of a stock portfolio. Investors can buy option puts for a fee (a premium), which gives them the right to have their stocks bought at the prearranged strike price, which they can do at any time of their choosing up to the expiration date of the option. That way, if the stock drops in price, they can exercise their option put and sell their stocks, not at the market price but at the strike price, or they can sell their option without the need to exercise it if its price goes up. Knowing the fixed amounts of the premium and strike price can help investors plan and protect their capital against the unknowns of the market. The downsides of this approach are that the cost of the premiums will decrease the rate of profits, and the fact that each standard option contract includes one hundred stocks at a time, a size that may not always be practical. Advanced traders may also hedge their portfolios using more complex techniques, such as actively trading commodity futures contracts (Sears 2019), which can help protect investors' capitals against market swings but require a good understanding of those types of derivative contracts.

- **Stop loss orders.** For those who trade within shorter time frames, such as swing traders, the volatility of the market may be much more relevant in their investment strategy. In such cases, setting stop orders in a consistent manner —such as trailing stop orders— can limit the losses if the market were to move in the opposite direction than the one they anticipated when they initiated their trades.

- **Portfolio monitoring.** Tracking market and investment trends to identify potential shifts and reversals —often with the help of charts with indicators that can aid in their technical analysis— can also help investors manage risk.

> When investors determine that the market may be going down they can, for instance, switch to buying bond ETFs, commodity ETFs, or defensive stocks instead of growth stocks as an attempt to shield their investment capital.

For beginners, a gradual approach in which they start investing small amounts of money, and only increase those amounts as they gain experience and feel more comfortable scaling up, may also help them test the waters and reduce the risks associated with transactions whose implications they do not yet fully understand.

Having risk management measures ready to be implemented can help investors think in advance of the potential actions they could take in response to adverse market scenarios, and be better prepared to protect the value of their stock portfolios.

6

UNDERSTANDING INVESTOR PSYCHOLOGY

Stock market psychology is a crucial part of the investment process, particularly when we consider that self-defeating patterns can make a well-thought-out investment strategy fail.

We often end up comparing our views about the prospects of stocks with those of others, even when the views of others are the ones reflected in the direction taken by the market, which is shaped by the collective behavior of other investors, making us doubt our own analyses and conclusions.

In other words, the trends observed in the stock market can be approached as the result of the actions of other investors, based on their aggregated perceptions about the likely financial performance of stocks in the future, regardless of the methods used to carry out their analyses.

In this context, John Maynard Keynes compared the stock market to "*a beauty contest where the winner is not the most beautiful contestant but the one whom the greatest number of people consider beautiful,*" which is in part caused by our imperfect grasp of reality (Soros 2003).

The effect of investors' reactions is also part of the assumptions of fundamental analysts. As Hayes explained, they believe that the market tends to over-react to bad and good news alike, resulting in price changes not aligned with the long-term fundamentals of a company, providing them with the opportunity to profit by buying stocks at discounted prices (2020).

If left unchecked, emotions can drive investors to make rash decisions that have the potential to create substantially detrimental effects on the performance of their portfolios and their investing experience in general, and even turn into a vicious cycle of actions and reactions.

Learning to identify the emotions underlying our investment decisions is thus a key first step to acknowledging their presence, and taking the necessary steps to manage them when they happen.

Steenbarger explains that, instead of attempting to overcome or suppress emotions, investors could benefit from learning to identify the emotions they experience and use them in productive ways, such as considering them as potential indicators in contrarian trades (2002).

The following section explains in more detail some of the different emotions experienced by stock market participants, which often affect the execution of their investment plans, and also shape their approach to key issues like timing the market and investing during recession periods.

COMMON EMOTIONS

Understanding the role of emotions in investors' financial decisions can go a long way in helping investors avoid costly mistakes in their stock market transactions. In that process, some emotions that are important for investors to identify, acknowledge, and carefully examine to account for their potential effect on their decision-making processes are included next.

Unrealistic Expectations

Many of us have heard the stories of investors who made fortunes in the stock market, and some expect to obtain similar levels of return when they invest in stocks. In practice, however, their situation may be different. A study conducted by Dalbar in 2001, and repeated in 2015, revealed that the average investor achieved a 5.32 percent return over seventeen years, in a period when the S&P 500 averaged 16.29 percent annually. When these investors do not see the returns they expected, this situation often makes them regard their stocks with suspicion, casting self-doubt, and often leading them to sell their stocks to buy the top performers instead. In many cases, they also keep searching for a better method to reach their expected levels of return, in what Van Tharp calls the quest for the "holy grail" of trading secrets, often looking at the trading methods developed by others instead of thinking independently and designing investing approaches that fit their own circumstances (2006).

Limited Patience

Long-term investments are more likely to provide gains than short-term speculation. However, when investors experience losses, they frequently tend to sell their stocks without giving them a chance to recover, even in cases when they would have been able to break even if they had simply waited long enough, or even sell their stocks for a profit down the road, provided they invested in solid companies that happened to be affected by broader market downturns. Unless an investor has an urgent need for hard cash, or has meaningful reasons to believe that the stock may not rebound within a reasonable period of time, the smart move in many such cases could have been to stick to their investment strategy. Sometimes investors also sell their best-performing stocks to lock in their profits, limiting the chances of those stocks to reach higher market prices.

Loss Aversion

Many investors experience fear and sell their stocks when their prices drop because they were not mentally prepared to weather the losses caused by price fluctuations, which are common in the stock market, particularly in the short term. The pressure to sell intensifies as stock prices sink deeper, causing investors to close their positions and lose a significant part of their investment capital. This is common because for many investors the losses feel much worse than the gains, and create the need to stop the source of their stress. The downside of this behavior lies in the fact that, by selling low, they give up on the chances of stock recovery, particularly in the case of stocks with temporary lows but with significant growth potential in the long run. However, if limiting losses before the stocks lose too much value is part of their trading strategy, then traders could benefit from executing their planned actions for such scenarios even when they may be otherwise inclined to wait.

Price Anchoring

Price anchoring is another important stock market emotion. It refers to the perception that the value of a stock is the one displayed at the moment an investor starts tracking it. Price declines are then perceived as opportunities to buy low, and price gains are interpreted as indications that the stock may be getting too expensive. This view may prevent investors from buying stocks with good prospects, or buying more, at a higher price than an investor previously bought them. This price fixation may also make investors buy the stocks of struggling companies at lower prices instead. If a similar perception is used in the analysis of market trends, taking the prices of indexes when they start tracking them as a reference, this may also distort their view of upcoming trends.

Peer Pressure

There is a tendency to agree with the opinion of the majority, even when a person would not have arrived at the same conclusions on their own. We are not immune to the influence of friends, neighbors, or family members when they talk about their opinions about the stock market or individual stocks. The same goes for financial commentators on TV, social media, people who got a prediction right before, and the many Internet sources posting information about stock trends. When investors base their trading decisions on the opinions of others, however, there is a reasonable chance that they may not have the same results because their circumstances are different, like the timing of their stock purchases and the specific behavior of the market during those periods.

Fear of Missing Out

One of the most basic rules of investing is to buy low and sell high, but buying high when there are good chances that the stock will go up even further also makes financial sense (O'Neil 2009). Accordingly, when investors hear of a promising stock whose price is quickly rising, many investors want to own it before its price goes higher. However, when this happens at times when the market is close to reaching its upper levels of resistance, or at the beginning of a distribution stage, then the expectations that such stocks will keep growing may not be fulfilled and investors' optimism may falter, causing them to sell even at a loss to purchase the latest rising stocks before those become too expensive. This creates a vicious cycle that gradually erodes participants' investment capital.

Investment Regret

Buyer's remorse also plays an important role in stock market psychology. This often comes into play when stock prices drop and investors perceive that they have made poor investment decisions, quickly forgetting the reasons that convinced them to purchase the stocks in the first place, which may lead them to sell their stocks to cut their losses. Given the fact that no investor can accurately and consistently predict how the market will move, investors will experience losses from time to time. However, those who expect to always be right may, when faced with a challenge, tend to believe that there is something wrong with their analytical skills or their investment strategy. This can erode their confidence as investors and limit their potential to participate in trades that, while contrarian in nature —at a time when most market participants do not yet see their advantage— may have promising growth prospects.

Financial Stress

The pressure to reach positive returns on an investment may be felt with particular intensity by those who are increasingly falling behind in their efforts to reach their financial goals, like those looking to retire maintaining a lifestyle not supported by their post-retirement levels of income, those burdened by high amounts of debt, or those who have already lost money on other investments. Such pressure may also come from peers or family members. This may prevent investors from carrying out their stock market analyses with the necessary peace of mind, since their decisions may be significantly influenced by a strong need for positive results, and make them more inclined to take on higher levels of risk not necessarily consistent with their risk tolerance levels.

Overreaction Tendency

When investors hear great news about a company, they may tend to feel overoptimistic, based on the belief that such news will have a positive impact on their stock prices, and such euphoria may cause them to buy such stocks even after their prices have considerably increased. The inverse can also happen, since negative news may result in extreme pessimism and give rise to concerns that cause investors to overreact, driving them to quickly sell their positions even at a loss. These overreaction tendencies can make investors lose money when the volatility ends up being short-lived, and prices return to levels near the ones they had before the disrupting news was released. If enough investors overreact in the same direction, like when there is market panic over a perceived or real threat, the disruptions to stock prices and their potential losses could be substantial.

Financial discipline is therefore crucial to the process of handling investing emotions. Successful investors understand stock market psychology, train themselves to identify their emotional impulses in response to market volatility, and evaluate them with a critical eye. Decisions to buy, sell, or hold stocks should be systematically informed by market analyses, and conscious investors will take the time to review their planned trades to ensure consistency with their overall investment strategy.

TIMING THE MARKET

Another important consideration is the attitude of investors toward the timing to enter and exit the stock market. As discussed in the market cycles section, if investors buy stocks during the accumulation stage, when their overall price is low, those stocks could provide substantial returns when the market reaches its distribution stage, as represented in Chart 2.

While identifying the right times to enter and exit the markets is important, this is not an easy process, so many investors do not even attempt to gain such understanding. Their approach in many cases is to use the dollar-cost average approach instead, which enables them to make regular stock purchases at different price levels, like monthly purchases based on a salary percentage, reducing the effect of market fluctuations over time. While dollar-cost averaging can reduce the level of risk associated with stock market volatility, it is not a proactive attempt to optimize returns.

When investors can correctly assess the stage in the market cycle at a given time, however, such understanding can make a substantial difference in the performance of their investments. As McAllen pointed out, investing mistakes are usually the result of two things: "*Either the wrong investment was purchased, or the investment was purchased at the wrong time... purchasing any investment at the wrong time is most always the recipe for loss*" (2012).

Investor psychology plays an important part in this process, since it requires a significant amount of discipline to stick with an investing strategy across market cycles. When the price of stocks has been dropping significantly, like during the markdown stage that precedes the accumulation stage, it may be counterintuitive to be among the first investors to start buying again.

Similarly, when prices are soaring, it may be easy to think that such a trend will continue, and avoid thinking about the transition to the markdown approach. Investors aware of these trends, however, may be on the lookout for signs of trend reversals and take timely corrective actions. In some cases, technical analysis may be able to help investors better understand stock market trends, particularly if they learn to use indicators and oscillators to spot potential trend reversals.

The use of trailing stop orders may be also useful for investors, since they allow them to place purchase orders for stocks when the stocks are dropping in price to be automatically bought, not right away, but once the trend reverses and their price has increased by a certain percentage or dollar amount in relation to their previous lows. Trailing orders can be also used to sell stocks; these orders become active when their upward trend reverses and their price has dropped by a certain amount or proportion.

Since these automated orders do not allow for the analysis of other trend indicators for confirmation, such as transaction volumes, investors could set alerts after certain conditions are met, and/or place trailing orders to buy or sell small amounts first, and then do a manual analysis to confirm the trend before trading more.

Making investment decisions in a way that differs from what the majority of investors are doing, or consider appropriate at the time, involves adopting a contrarian approach, which may seem counterintuitive and is not easy to do. However, as Warren Buffet pointed out, "*a simple rule dictates my buying: Be fearful when others are greedy, and be greedy when others are fearful*" (2008).

The more investors understand market cycles and trends, the better prepared they will be to use that knowledge to their advantage and make informed investing decisions, acknowledging that some of those decisions may not always be aligned with their conscious or subconscious emotions.

INVESTING DURING RECESSIONS

Investing during a recession can raise fears among investors, particularly because of the uncertainty about the health of the economy and its unforeseen effects, including the time it may take for the market to recover. However, investing during a recession can also be a profitable endeavor, particularly for those entering the stock market at its accumulation stage with a long-time horizon.

The stock market usually experiences a substantial hit during those periods, with stocks losing a high proportion of their market value. Such circumstances, however, also represent an investment opportunity to buy stocks at a deep discount price, particularly the ones of solid companies with the potential for a substantial upswing when the market eventually recovers.

New investors with cash reserves would be especially well positioned to take advantage of recession conditions, buying stocks when prices are low and holding on to them at least until the economy recovers. Those who are already invested may have to wait for the market to recover, unless they opted to place stop orders and were able to close their positions before prices dropped too much.

Something else that some investors consider when stock prices are low is buying stock replacements —option calls that are deep in the money, as long as their percentage to break even is low, for example less than 2 percent, or have a negative percentage. This resembles making a substantial down payment for the right to buy a given number of stocks at a later date, which can be up to two or three years in the future, without requiring investors to pay the full cost until the option is exercised, allowing investors to leverage their purchasing power while the price of stocks in the market is low. Investors, however, would need to sell or exercise the options they hold before they expire.

For investors with greater risk tolerances, experience, and confidence in their market analyses, using margin to buy stocks when prices are low is another alternative to leverage their purchasing power. At the time of this writing, Robinhood was offering margin rates as low as 2.5 percent, and M1 Finance's rates were 2 percent for its M1 Plus members. If used, this approach should be considered with great caution, since the risks of margin investment are higher than with cash, and there are no guarantees that the stocks will rebound or recover to the levels they had before the recession.

Different industries are affected differently during a financial crisis, since each sector has its own market dynamics. Even though each recession is unique, there may be certain commonalities. Here are some examples of the likely influence of recessions on certain economic sectors:

- **Consumer staples.** Essential businesses like grocery stores and consumer goods remain active during recession times. People still need them, even though the range of products available and their overall volume of sales may be reduced. The elasticity of the demand, and the availability of close substitutes for certain products, are also important factors to consider. While the upswing of stocks in this sector may not be the greatest once the economy recovers, these stocks may provide some resilience to a portfolio while the recession lasts.

- **Utilities.** These stocks were among the best-performing ones on the S&P 500 index in the first two months of the COVID-19 pandemic (NYT 2020). While not much growth is usually associated with utility companies, some of them may offer important dividends even during the crisis.

- **Precious metals.** During the 2008 financial crisis, gold had a historic rise in its value, as did silver during the COVID-19 pandemic. As an alternative to actually buying the precious metals, or the futures contracts associated with them, there are other investment vehicles, like precious metal ETFs, which people can use to invest while the stock market is down.

- **Technology**. While technology stocks may show significant levels of price fluctuation, such volatility also represents an opportunity. If bought at a time when they are already close to their market bottoms, their upswing potential once the market recovers could be substantial. Some stocks, however, may have their own dynamics not always related to their sector.

The cyclical nature of the U.S. economy can also help investors understand market fluctuations. The last cycle had a downturn from 2007–2009, and then there was an upswing between 2010–2019. There are also off-cycle economic disruptions, such as the recession created by the COVID-19 pandemic. One of the best ways for investors to face these cycles may be to stick to their investment strategy, particularly if they consider a long-term investing horizon, which can add resilience to a portfolio.

While buying shares when the stock market is at a low point makes sense, there is no easy way to see if the prices will keep dropping or assess how long it will take until the market recovers. To address this uncertainty, one option frequently considered in these cases is dollar-cost averaging, which involves buying shares at regular intervals to average the purchase prices out.

Because the stakes are high, even experts tend to get cautious during recessions. There are no guarantees, and even the apparently most stable stocks involve some level of risk. That is why defining an investment plan and staying the course over recession periods is important, since it can counteract the tendency to exit the market at the wrong time because of market fears.

Like in many other areas of business, and in personal endeavors as well, adequate preparation is crucial for successful investments. A combination of general knowledge of market fluctuations and careful research on the investments under consideration are key aspects of such preparation.

7

LEVERAGING OPTIONS TRADING

This chapter explains the basics of options contracts, including the contractual nature of options as derivative financial products, their basic characteristics and features, the use of options calls and puts depending on the anticipated direction of the market, and the use of indicators such as the Greeks to analyze the price, the risks, and the potential behavior of options.

The information in this chapter is expected to serve as a brief introduction to the topic, addressing only the essential characteristics of option contracts, since this is an extensive area of knowledge that could be better addressed in a separate book. However, given the importance of options in an investment strategy, understanding their basic characteristics can be helpful for investors.

Before getting into the details, it is crucial to understand that options involve risks and are not suitable for all investors. Prior to buying or selling options, investors should read a copy of the document "*Characteristics and Risks of Standardized Options*," which, along with the Options Clearing Corporation (OCC) Prospectus, is available from the OCC and brokerage firms. The learning resources subsection of this chapter includes hyperlinks to these and other relevant websites.

OPTIONS CONTRACTS

Options are derivative financial instruments that can be applied to different investment vehicles such as stocks, ETFs, bonds, currencies, and commodities, among others. In this case, the focus will be on stock options, as an extension of stock investing strategies.

Options are not company shares but contracts that investors can buy or sell for a given price (called the premium), which, once bought, give the buyer the right to buy or sell a given number of stocks at a fixed price (called the strike price) within the time frame agreed on in the contract. As such, their price is based on the expected market value of the underlying security at a predefined time in the future.

Options have an expiration date, ranging from a few days to up to three years. If no action is taken within the option's validity period, however, then the option becomes void. Options cannot be exercised or traded after their expiration date; whatever value they had is lost at that time.

While the term *contract* reflects the nature of options, in practice there are no contracts to read or documents to sign. The terms and conditions that govern those trades are presented during the account setup process, when an investor opts in to conduct option trades.

Once purchased, the holders of option contracts usually sell their options when the options reach a price that enables them to obtain a profit, if the value of the option moves in a favorable direction. Selling the options held is the most common occurrence, since their volatility enables investors to profit from their price variation without the need to actually buy the underlying stocks.

If an investor wants to buy (exercise) the underlying stock at the agreed strike price, there are two styles: American and European. American-style option holders can exercise their right to buy the underlying stocks early, from the moment they own the option until its expiration date. With European-style options, investors may exercise their right to buy the underlying stocks only during the option's expiration day. Stock options offered by U.S. stockbrokers are American-style.

Standard options are traded in packages of 100 shares per contract. Unlike stocks, where investors can buy any number of shares of a company, or fractional shares in some cases, what options traders buy is numbers of contracts, and each contract can be sold or exercised separately.

The ability to trade options is not enabled by default when people open brokerage accounts; they have to be indicated in the preferences or explicitly requested. Once options are enabled, there are different access levels. The one that allows buying option calls and option puts is level 2. Buying option calls allows investors to buy deep-in-the-money long-term option calls as stock substitutes, while buying option puts can help investors hedge their portfolios.

CALLS AND PUTS

Investors can buy and sell options calls and puts. Here is a brief explanation of the four main types of options trades available:

- **Buying Option Calls.** Buying a call (buy to open), by paying a premium, gives option call holders the right, but not the obligation, to exercise the option call and buy the underlying stock at the strike price. Once it has been bought, the call can be resold (sell to close) to other traders in the market to exit this position, without the need to exercise the contract.

- **Selling Option Calls.** Selling a call (sell to open) enables the call sellers to collect the premium, and creates the obligation to sell the underlying stocks at the strike price, whenever the buyer or the call holder decide to exercise their option. If the seller of the call already owns the underlying stocks, these trades are called covered calls. If the seller does not own the stock, these trades are called naked calls and would require the seller to buy stocks in the marketplace when the calls are exercised. Selling naked calls is particularly risky because there is no limit to the potential losses for the seller.

- **Buying Option Puts.** Buying a put (buy to open) by paying a premium gives put holders the right, but not the obligation, to exercise the option put and sell their stocks at the strike price. Once it has been bought, the option put can be resold (sell to close) to other traders in the market to exit this position, without the need to exercise the contract.

- **Selling Option Puts.** Selling a put (sell to open) enables put sellers to collect the premium, and creates the obligation for them to buy the underlying stocks from the buyer or the holder of the option put at the strike price, whenever the holder of the put decides to exercise their option to sell, so the put seller needs to have funds reserved for that purchase.

Because the strike price that investors pay to buy option calls and puts are known to them in advance, the limit of what they could lose if the market were to go in the opposite direction from what they originally expected would be limited to the cost of the premium they paid. The differences between options calls and puts are explained in greater detail next.

Option Calls

One of the most basic types of options trades is buying option calls, which function under a similar logic as when buying stocks. Buying option calls works under the assumption that the price of the underlying securities will go up (a long position) during the time the option is held. If an option contract is bought and exercised (by paying both the premium and then the strike price), the buyer gets the number of stocks specified in the contract. If an option is bought and held, the call holder keeps the right to trade it or exercise it at a later time, up to the expiration date.

If the price of the underlying stock is then higher than the strike price, the call option is "in the money." If the price of the stock is lower than the strike price, the call option is then "out of the money." There is no obligation to exercise option calls bought, and holders could let a contract expire if they see no value in trading it, but will then lose the premium they paid.

When buying an option call, one key variable to evaluate the price of an option contract is the "percentage to break even," which enables investors to quickly assess the difference between different options contracts. The percentage to break even is calculated by adding the strike price plus the premium, and then subtracting that amount from the current stock price. For instance, one option contract may need an 80 percent increase in the underlying stock's market price to break even, and can be usually be bought for a relatively low premium, while another contract may need to see an increase of only 2 percent in the underlying stock's market price to break even, but may involve a higher premium cost. However, if the expiration date of the latter is two years ahead or more, and the stock price were to grow more than 2 percent in that period, the investor would benefit from trading this option, assuming that the underlying stock has not experienced a substantial increase in recent periods, such as the ones associated with temporary peaks following events like quarterly earnings, short-term bubbles, short squeeze rallies, acquisition plans, or other disruptive behaviors that exacerbate its volatility levels.

In practical ways, buying option calls can be understood as an extension of buying stocks, as stock replacements, in the sense that these contracts could translate into the possession of shares in the underlying company. For instance, investors that want to buy 100 shares of company XYZ but only have enough capital to buy 50 shares can buy an option call, and consider the strike price as their down payment. The investors can then pay the remaining amount at a later time, once they have saved or secured enough money to exercise their option, without worrying about the price of the stock going up, as long as it is at or before the option's expiration date. Dividends, if any, are issued to the owners of the underlying stock, not to the option holders.

When selling options calls, the percentage to break even is transformed into the chance of profit percentage. To sell calls (covered calls), traders can buy the required number of shares, unless they already own them, and then sell an option for investors to buy those shares at a certain strike price. If the option is sold and exercised, then the issuer of the call loses the underlying stock but collects both the premium and the strike price. If the option is sold but not exercised, then the issuer of the call keeps both the premium and the underlying stock.

An options strategy explained in Ally Invest's *Options Playbook* consists of buying long-term option calls that are deep in the money —those with more than nine months until their expiration date and up to two or three years, to be sold or exercised before they expire— like long-term equity anticipation securities (LEAPS), particularly those with a Delta of 0.8 or greater, which can be used as stock substitutes (Overby 2009).

To reduce the level of risk when using LEAPS, investors could choose to limit their trades to option calls with a percentage to break even around 2 percent or less, and even better if such percentage were to be negative, which would mean that the total cost of the option (premium plus strike price) is lower than the market price of the underlying stock. Option calls with such percentages to break even normally have high premiums and low strike prices, making it more likely that those options will expire in the money, enabling investors to profit if the price of the underlying stocks goes up. With this type of option contract, the risk is kept at a level similar to what an investor would experience when buying the underlying stocks.

If the underlying stock experienced substantial growth in price and the Delta is high —as discussed in the next subsection— selling the option call may be more profitable than exercising it, since investors can then achieve a greater rate of return in proportion to their invested capital without needing to use the full amount of money that would be required to exercise their option calls.

Table 1. Relevant Information When Buying Option Calls					
Expiration Date	Current Share Price*	Strike Price	Premium ($)**	Total Cost ($)***	% To Break Even
Jan 24, 2020	38.96	46.00	0.02	46.02	18.12%
		42.00	0.03	42.03	7.88%
		38.00	1.16	39.16	0.51%
		34.50	4.30	38.80	0.41%
		31.00	7.98	38.98	0.05%
Jul 17, 2020	38.96	49.00	0.06	49.06	25.92%
		40.00	1.41	41.41	6.29%
		32.00	7.05	39.05	0.23%
		25.00	14.00	39.00	0.10%
		20.00	19.00	39.00	0.10%
Jan 15, 2021	38.96	50.00	0.21	50.21	28.88%
		40.00	2.06	42.06	7.96%
		35.00	4.78	39.78	2.10%
		25.00	13.88	38.88	-0.21%****
		15.00	23.85	38.85	-0.28%
Jan 21, 2022	**38.96**	55.00	0.35	55.35	42.07%
		45.00	1.47	46.47	19.28%
		35.00	5.30	40.30	3.44%
		28.00	**9.60**	**37.60**	**-3.49%**
		20.00	18.73	38.73	-0.59%

* Reference date considered: December 26, 2019.

** This cost is per share, so these amounts will need to be multiplied by 100 (for one contract).

*** Total cost is the breakeven point and includes the strike price plus the premium, per share, to get ownership of the underlying shares in the options contract, without considering potential transaction fees.
**** When buying option calls, negative percentages to break even indicate that the strike price of the option contract plus the premium, if exercised right away, would be less than the market price of the stock.

Table 1 provides an example of the basic information involved in buying an option call. In this scenario, the investor has the opportunity to select an option with an expiration date in the future, and examine the different choices available to find one with a low percentage of growth needed to break even. The investor decides to buy one call contract, which contains 100 stocks (if exercised), with an expiration date of January 21, 2022, at a strike price of $28.00, paying a premium of $9.60 for that right. The cost of this transaction would be $960 when buying this option call, plus $2,800 when exercising it, unless the investor decides to sell the option without exercising it.

Option Puts

Another type of options trade is buying option puts, which is often favored by investors who work under the assumption that the price of the underlying securities may go down (a short position) during the time in which the put option contract they hold is valid. Table 2 illustrates this situation.

Table 2. Relevant Information When Buying Option Puts					
Expiration Date	Current Share Price*	Strike Price	Premium ($)**	Total Return ($)***	% To Break Even
Jan 24, 2020	38.96	46.00	7.60	38.40	-1.44%
		42.00	3.55	38.45	-1.31%
		38.00	0.47	37.53	-3.67%
		34.50	0.05	34.45	-11.58%
		31.00	0.02	30.98	-20.48%
Jul 17, 2020	38.96	49.00	11.15	37.85	-2.85%
		40.00	3.38	36.62	-6.01%
		37.00	1.82	35.18	-9.70%
		32.00	0.54	31.46	-19.25%
		20.00	0.03	19.97	-48.74%
Jan 15, 2021	38.96	50.00	12.50	37.50	-3.75%
		40.00	4.58	35.42	-9.09%
		35.00	2.15	32.85	-15.68%
		25.00	0.36	24.64	-36.76%
		15.00	0.05	14.95	-61.63%
Jan 21, 2022	**38.96**	55.00	18.53	36.47	-6.39%
		45.00	**10.00**	**35.00**	**-10.16%**
		35.00	3.83	31.17	-19.99%
		28.00	1.60	26.40	-32.24%
		20.00	0.52	19.48	-50.00%

* Reference date considered: December 26, 2019.

** This cost is per share, so these amounts will need to be multiplied by 100 (for one contract).

*** Total return is the breakeven point, which includes the strike price minus the premium, per share, the amount investors would receive for their stock, if they exercise the option (not considering transaction fees).

Option puts work in an inverse way to option calls. Buying option puts can act as insurance in case the price of the underlying stocks or ETFs goes down. Some traders also use them as a shorting speculative strategy when they believe the stock market prices will drop.

Table 2 provides an example of the basic information involved in buying an option put. In this scenario, the investor has come to the conclusion that the price of XYZ may go down and wants to balance the cost and expiration date of the option puts. The investor decides to buy one put contract with an expiration date of January 21, 2022, at a strike price of $45.00, paying a premium of $10.00 for that right. The costs of this transaction for the put buyer would be $1,000 when buying the put option (buy to open), and would receive $4,500 for the sale of 100 shares of XYZ (for one contract) when that put option is exercised, unless the put is resold or allowed to expire. This trade could prove beneficial to the investor if the stock price were to drop at least 10.16 percent.

When it comes to options, the option calls and put chains data presented by many stockbrokers in their online platforms could in some cases be overwhelming, with many variations to accommodate the different needs of traders. While some people need sophisticated option schemes, others do not need all that information. For beginning investors, simplicity in the way of presenting option pricing information is important to avoid confusion. Robinhood, for instance, presents key information like the percentage to break even and the chance of profit percentage in a very clear format, avoiding the need for offline calculations and facilitating the visual screening process.

PRICING INDICATORS

In addition to the percentage to break even, the Greeks are also important options indicators that can be used to help guide investment decisions involving options, including option pricing, stability, and risks. The values of these variables are dynamic, so the probabilities will change on a continuous basis, depending on the market conditions.

One of the most important Greek letters is Delta. This is a measure that reflects how much the price of an option is expected to move in relation to the change in the price of the underlying stock. The value of Delta goes from 0 to 1 in options calls, with values closer to 1 for in-the-money options, and closer to 0 for the ones out of the money. For instance, if the price of the underlying stock increases by $1, the price of an option call with a Delta of 0.8 will increase by $0.80. In options with a Delta of close to 0, the change in the stock price should not affect the options price by much. The range in option puts is negative, going from 0 to -1.

A related Greek letter is Gamma, which refers to the level of responsiveness in option prices to changes in the value of the underlying stock. Gamma values are usually higher for options that are in the money.

High Gamma values indicate that the value of the option could change significantly in response to small variations in the price of the stock, while low Gamma values indicate greater stability in the forecast of option prices.

Another aspect of options trading is time decay, which can be assessed with the help of Theta. This Greek letter indicates the amount the option calls and puts will decrease for each day that passes, as the option expiration date gets closer. Options that are out of the money are the ones likely to experience the most significant losses as the time left is reduced.

Other Greek letters used in options trading are Vega, which indicates changes in the value of an option based on changes in the volatility levels of the underlying stock, and Rho, which indicates changes in interest rates, which may be particularly relevant for bond ETF options.

Readers interested in learning more about these and other options topics may want to consult other available resources, such as the following:

○ *Characteristics and Risks of Standardized Options.* Prior to buying or selling an option, investors should read this document, available at https://www.theocc.com/Company-Information/Documents-and-Archives/Publications

○ The Options Clearing Corporation (OCC) *Prospectus*, available at https://www.theocc.com

○ Courses at the Options Institute Online Learning Center, many of which are available for free, available at https://ww2.cboe.com/education/online-courses

○ *Options Playbook*. Electronic resource, available at www.optionsplaybook.com/options-introduction/

○ *Options for Beginners*. Online course taught by Lucas Downey. Investopedia Academy, available at: https://academy.investopedia.com/products/options-for-beginners

8

MAKING USE OF AVAILABLE RESOURCES

The overall tendency of the stock market is to grow over time. While more than half of U.S. households currently own stocks, there is also a significant proportion of the population that does not. One of the main reasons for this is the limited knowledge of how the stock market works.

This chapter includes key resources available for beginners. They include a curated compilation of online resources, books, magazines, videos, tools, advisory services, and other resources that can help new investors learn more about the stock market, and strengthen their ability to make informed investment decisions, thus improving their chances of being successful in their trades.

ONLINE RESOURCES

The Internet offers a wealth of data about the stock market, so much that oftentimes it becomes difficult to navigate it efficiently to find the right information. Below is a hand-picked list of online resources with information useful for beginning investors, including financial websites, educational videos, stock market news outlets, and other resources such as stock screeners.

Financial Websites

- **Investopedia**. This website is one of the most comprehensive repositories of articles, financial definitions, tools, and other content related to the stock market, written in a beginner-friendly style. Its website offers a stock market simulator, a useful feature that allows users to record pretend purchases (paper trading) and monitor how they perform over time, among other resources.

- **The Balance**. This website has a section about investing for beginners, which includes many articles on financial investing, providing general information on the stock market, fundamental finance concepts, ways of investing, the difference between different investment vehicles, recommendations to develop an investment strategy, and steps to come up with an actionable investment plan.

- **Bankrate**. This website includes a section on stock market basics, which provides a huge breadth of personal finance information. It includes information on financial markets, investing, mortgages, loans, commercial interest rates, and more. It also has a section that serves as a good explainer of the stock market, including what it is, how it works, and what the rewards and risks of stock market investing are, as well as giving a variety of investing tips for beginners.

- **Morningstar**. This website provides analysts' ratings of stocks, ETFs, and mutual funds, a stock market barometer, investment research, articles about the stock market, news, and information on index trends. It also hosts a specialized database of financial data, along with software tools to process such data, which can help investors, financial advisors, and asset managers.

Educational Videos

- *TED Ed: How Does the Stock Market Work?* This short video is a great educational resource. It quickly goes over the basics of what the stock market is, how it started and grew, how it works now, and how people can invest in it to make more money, not just those with significant financial resources but also regular individuals who can easily become small investors. [Link: www.youtube.com/watch?v=p7HKvqRI_Bo]

- *Warren Buffett: How to Invest for Beginners.* Warren Buffett is one of the most successful investors in the world. In this video, he discusses seven factors that have guided his investment approach over the years, focusing on finding companies with great long-term prospects that can be bought at fair prices, in sectors that the investor understands, guided by facts associated with the financial prospects of a company rather than by emotions. [Link: www.youtube.com/watch? v=yRr0_gJ-3mI]

- *Stock Market for Beginners: How to Invest (Step by Step).* This video explains the main concepts surrounding investing in the stock market, providing a broad overview that new investors may find helpful. It also addresses the main approaches to investing, stockbrokers, and types of investment accounts, among many other relevant topics. [Link: www.youtube.com/watch?v=dFAiChOmoGI]

- *Stock Market for Beginners.* This video explains how the stock market works, going over a variety of stock market basics and answering ten of the most popular questions from beginners about stocks, including what stocks are, how to buy stocks, what investors normally consider when buying stocks, index funds versus stocks, how to make money with stocks, best-case and worst-case scenarios, and taxes, among other related topics. [Link: www.youtube.com/watch?v=-eXAGjPPz4k]

Stock Market News

- **Yahoo! Finance.** This website is not just a stock-related news portal but a place where users can access, for free, a huge amount of information about what is happening in the stock market and about individual securities. It offers real-time stock quotes, historical data, company profiles, access to stock performance charts with useful indicators, and the ability to create simulated stock portfolios and watchlists and track stock portfolios across multiple linked accounts with stockbrokers. There are also premium paid features. The mobile app also provides alerts on market news and portfolio events.

- **MarketWatch**. This is a specialized provider of financial and stock market news, analysis, stock market data, and general investment advice articles. It also provides research tools such as stock screening, price alerts, and upcoming initial public offerings (IPOs), among other useful information for investors. Its mobile app also provides alerts on general stock market trends on a regular basis.

- **CNBC**. As a national business news channel, its TV channel and online portal are an important source of news and commentaries related to the financial sector and the stock market. It includes specialized programming, like the popular show *Mad Money* with Jim Cramer. Many of the online articles available for free on its website also includes short video clips from its regular TV programs, providing multimedia-rich content that is frequently updated.

- **Stockbrokers Newsfeeds**. Most stockbrokers offer aggregated newsfeeds from multiple third-party services related to the specific stocks being researched by an investor.

Training Courses

There are many online courses that can help beginning investors learn more about the stock market. Here are some options to consider when exploring potential training courses.

- **Investopedia Academy**. This platform offers a list of courses taught by experts in the field, some of them being former Wall Street traders. Many of its courses were developed for beginners, like Investing for Beginners, Technical Analysis, Fundamental Analysis, and Options for Beginners. It occasionally offers discounts, particularly during the shopping holidays.

- **Courses on Udemy**. This platform includes many training courses on the stock market, including Investing in Stocks: The Complete Course by Steve Ballinger, which is taught by an investor, and The Complete Foundation Stock Trading Course by Mohsen Hassan, which may be helpful for those interested in learning to invest with short time frames from a trader's point of view.

- **College Offerings**. These include Stocks, Bonds, and Investing, by Matt Crabtree, offered by the University of Central Florida's Continuing Education program, and Behavioral Investing by

Vaidya Nathan, offered by the Indian School of Business on Coursera.

- **Online Trading Academy** (OTA). This provider offers a free class that can be followed by other online modules like fundamental principles of investing, OTA's core strategy to understand market timing, and investing strategies, as part of its stocks program.

- **Courses on Skillshare.** There are brief courses on this platform, like Investing Basics for Millennials by Lindsay Marsh, and Understanding Stocks by Business Casual.

- **Investing 101**. This website offers its Stock Market Course for Beginners, which covers many different topics of interest for new investors, and includes a research tool, exercises, and a virtual trading account to practice with.

Other Resources

- **Stock Screeners.** These allow investors to filter stocks based on different criteria they select, such as performance metrics, market capitalizations, dividend yields, sectors and industries, countries, analyst recommendations, earnings per share, candlestick shapes, etc. Some popular stock screeners are FinViz, Macrotrends, StockRover, TradingView, and the ones provided by online brokers.

- **Online Brokers**. Brokerage companies usually have significant educational resources for beginners. These include articles explaining the basic investing terms, types of orders, charts, stock market news, analyst reports and recommendations from specialized sources like SmartConsensus, Thomson Reuters, and Credit Suisse, among many others. By signing up for a free account, investors can access the resources offered by their online platforms and mobile apps, which can be also configured to provide alerts when the price of stocks in a portfolio or watchlist changes.

- **Whitepapers**. There are many whitepapers that can provide useful information for investors. These are available from different online sources and usually can be accessed after users enter their email addresses. Some examples include Jim Cramer's "25 Rules for Investing," published by The Street (2018); and "The Market Answer Key: Big Money" by Bodner and Downey, from MapSignals (2020).

BOOKS AND MAGAZINES

Before investors start buying financial securities in the stock market, it is important that they understand how the stock market works, and define an investment strategy. The following books can be helpful for new investors to further strengthen their understanding of the stock market:

- *Trade Your Way to Financial Freedom* by Van Tharp. This book provides a series of steps for investors to develop a model according to their specific circumstances, with actionable measures and examples, facilitating an understanding of stock market behavior, risk management, position sizing, and investors' psychology, among many other topics.

- *How to Make Money in Stocks: A Winning System in Good Times and Bad* by William O'Neil. This book provides an organized way of combining the analysis of quantitative and qualitative factors associated with market movements, along with information from technical analysis.

- *Berkshire Hathaway Letters to Shareholders* by Warren Buffett. This collection of letters from one of the most successful investors provides educational value and can help investors understand the value of investing for the long term, and the importance of not fixating on the temporary setbacks created by market volatility.

- *The Little Book That Still Beats the Market* by Joel Greenblatt. This book explains the basics of how the stock market works and introduces readers to fundamental principles that are crucial to being a successful stock investor. It also explains the investment strategy of buying shares of companies that are undervalued but have above-average prospects.

- *A Beginner's Guide to the Stock Market: Everything You Need to Start Making Money Today* by Matthew Kratter. This book can help new investors understand the practical aspects of investing in stocks, like opening a brokerage account, tips to identify profitable stocks, and advice to avoid the pitfalls and mistakes that beginners usually make when they start trading stocks.

- *The Little Book of Common Sense Investing* by John Bogle. New investors could benefit from understanding the advantages of broad diversification when planning their investment strategy. This book introduces new investors to index funds, which involve low fees and seek to obtain levels of return similar to the ones of market indexes such as the S&P 500.

- *Charting and Technical Analysis* by Fred McAllen. This book provides an introduction to market trends, which can be particularly useful in helping new investors define their investment strategy. It also provides an overview of stock chart analysis, which can help investors identify stock patterns and the best times to conduct their stock market transactions.

- *The Psychology of Trading: Tools and Techniques for Minding the Markets* by Brett Steenbarger. This book provides insights into stock market emotions, helping investors learn how to identify them and use them in productive ways instead of suppressing them. New investors may find this helpful to supplement the technical aspects of their trading.

- *Investments* by Zvi Bodie, Alex Kane, and Alan Marcus. People looking for a more comprehensive textbook that can provide them with a solid foundation on financial investment vehicles, security analysis, investing strategies, portfolio management, debt instruments, company valuations, and derivatives, among many other related topics, may find this book useful.

- *How I Invest My Money: Finance Experts Reveal How They Save, Spend, and Invest*, edited by Joshua Brown and Brian Portnoy. The way investors and financial experts invest their own money, as opposed to the recommendations they issue for their clients or the criteria they use to manage other people's wealth, is reflected in this collection of twenty-five stories about money and values.

Financial Magazines

Financial magazines include articles and other pieces of information that can help investors stay informed about market trends, learn about business leaders, and discover new investment niches. They also feature stories of emerging companies and commentaries about their long-term growth expectations. The following magazines can offer valuable information for new investors:

- **Forbes.** Published eight times a year, with two combined editions and special issues, this magazine includes articles about the stock market, information about successful business leaders, and articles of emerging companies with commentaries that offer a broader perspective on the potential challenges that such companies may face, including their competition.

- **Fortune.** This magazine, published monthly with three combined issues, features select business and economic news, and provides investment guidance, rankings of companies with top revenues, and information about the leaders of the most successful companies and their tactics.

- **Kiplinger's Personal Finance.** This monthly magazine provides financial articles on market trends, emerging sectors, market cycles, interviews with financial leaders, and investing for retirement, as well as other information related to stocks, bonds, funds, ETFs, etc.

- **Barron's.** As investors become more experienced and able to understand more technical stock market terminology, they can also consider this weekly newspaper-style publication with short articles, insider activity, and stock purchases by large investors, among other relevant data.

- **Bloomberg Businessweek.** This weekly magazine offers news related to the business world and the stock market, analyses about what may be expected for the week ahead, and articles about the strategies of business leaders and successful companies, including startups.

- **ESG Magazine.** This digital publication, issued quarterly by Responsible Investor, provides free access to registered subscribers. Its focus is on news and resources related to the environmental, social, and governance aspects of investing in the stock market.

ADVISORY SERVICES

This section explains the roles of financial advisors, wealth managers, and stock advisory services, which can provide specialized information to guide investors' decisions.

- **Financial Advisors.** As previously discussed, investors can benefit from personalized expert advice to develop their investment plans provided by licensed financial advisors, who assist their clients to develop their investment strategy, determine their optimal asset allocations, find securities aligned with their investment goals, and identify potential pitfalls throughout the process. It is important to understand that while some advisors receive commissions from the sale of the products they sell to their clients, like mutual funds, others are fee-only registered investment advisors (RIAs), which have the fiduciary responsibility to act in the best interest of their clients. Many stockbrokers also have registered representatives and consultants among their staff; these professionals can carry out analyses of current investments, offer portfolio building strategies, issue investment recommendations, and execute trades.

- **Wealth Managers.** These specialists focus on investing and growing the financial assets of investors while managing the risks associated with such investments. This service is mostly used by large institutional investors, since for small investors this function is often carried out by financial advisors, who also offer financial planning, retirement planning, tax advice, etc. Wealth managers can be firms or financial specialists working independently.

Stock Advisory Services

There are different approaches to stock picking, and some of them require comprehensive analyses. To facilitate this process for investors, there are specialized companies whose business is analyzing stocks and sharing their analyses, findings, and recommendations with their clients, usually as part of paid memberships. Some of these services are included below.

- **The Motley Fool.** This company has different advisory service packages. One of its most popular services is Stock Advisor, which issues two new stock picks every month, and keeps an updated list of its top ten stock recommendations. Another of its services is called Rule Breakers.

- **Investor's Business Daily.** This service is based on a digital subscription that allows investors to access top stock pick recommendations, stock ratings, market analyses, and many other resources. These recommendations are based on its CAN SLIM investing system (O'Neil 2009).

- **Zacks Investment Research.** This service provides lists of stocks, ranked according to their chances of performing well according to the service's own methodology, research reports, and stock screeners, among others. It includes several plans for investors with different needs.

- **Seeking Alpha.** This service is based on a paid membership that provides lists of top-rated stocks, investment ideas, stock ratings and analysis, a stock screening tool, and a related-stocks feature, among many others, in addition to free crowdsourced articles.

- **MapSignals.** This is a service that finds the stocks that large Wall Street firms —whose massive purchases and sales of stocks oftentimes drive their prices up or down— are acquiring, and seeks to replicate their success by identifying when such moves take place. It also issues a free newsletter with links to informative articles on its website about market trends.

- **Wanderer Financial.** This is an advisory service that provides estimates of likely market moves, including alerts with recommended purchase price ranges, growth estimates, and stop loss levels in case stock prices were to move in the opposite direction than the one forecasted.

- **All Star Charts.** This advisory service advises investors on likely market moves indicated by the technical analysis of stock charts, through weekly email newsletters, quarterly research reports, monthly calls, specific chart requests, and other resources for investors.

Even if investors do not subscribe to these services, in some cases it could be beneficial to sign up for their free email lists, which often contain valuable information and article links, along with potential discounts on their services, particularly during the shopping holidays.

While every person has a different learning style, the resources included in this chapter can serve as starting points for investors to continue learning. These would be particularly helpful when used in combination, since multiple approaches can enhance investors' knowledge through exposure to different ways of investing in stocks, and assist them in developing strategies with unique combinations of factors, according to their own preferences, goals, and risk-tolerance levels.

9

GETTING READY TO INVEST

Having addressed broader stock market considerations, this chapter will discuss the practical aspects of investing, like selecting a stockbroker and opening a brokerage account, making the appropriate selections from the many alternatives available, understanding order types and when each of them may be appropriate to use, and knowing the basic elements to consider when preparing an investment plan.

SELECTING A STOCKBROKER

There are many online stockbrokers, also referred to as broker dealers, available for investors. Some of the most popular ones include TD Ameritrade, E*Trade, Charles Schwab, Merrill Edge, Fidelity Investments, Interactive Brokers, Ally Invest, Webull, and Robinhood, among many others.

Stockbrokers used to require minimum investment amounts to open a brokerage account, but many of them now allow the option to open accounts without minimums. Some stockbrokers like TD Ameritrade, Merrill Edge, and E*Trade sometimes even offer promotions that include cashback rewards for qualifying deposits made within a few weeks after opening a brokerage account.

Since October 2019, almost all stockbrokers have stopped charging commissions for online stock trades. After Charles Schwab slashed its commissions, the others followed suit. This was very good news for stock investors, who previously had to pay between $5 and $8 per trade, or more.

Some criteria to consider when selecting a stockbroker include the overall financial stability of the company; its track record, user base, and target audience; the way the information about stocks and their performance is presented to the user, so they can quickly visualize the information to help them with their trades without being overwhelmed by excessive data; assessing their potential hidden fees, since nowadays most offer free trades but some still charge fees for certain transactions; the types of orders available for trades, which in some cases could limit the execution of some investment strategies; the ability to allow uninterrupted trading; the information they provide about stocks, such as analysts' ratings and recommendations; the accessibility of key statistics like earnings per share, P/E ratios, and dividend yields; the ability to display charts with trends and indicator overlays; and the ability to select alerts to receive notifications when certain events or milestones are reached.

How relevant each of these factors is depends on their intended use by each investor. For people who prefer fundamental analysis, for instance, the ability to see detailed statistics would be important, in the same way that charts with the ability to add multiple indicator overlays may be important for those who rely on technical analysis. For people looking for a platform that is easy to understand and who do not need sophisticated features, Robinhood's smartphone app is very intuitive and one of the easiest for beginning investors to use.

Even if a stockbroker did not have the ideal combination of features, if some missing features are readily available from alternative sites, such as Yahoo Finance or Morningstar, for example, then these alternative platforms could be considered as part of an investor's research strategy.

There are also stockbrokers with specific features for specialized users. For instance, users who intend to use algorithmic trading could use a stockbroker such as Interactive Brokers, which allows this type of trading in addition to providing regular stock brokerage services, or Alpaca Markets, which offers a commission-free trading platform for people to use their algorithms.

Other platforms, such as Acorns, allow users to link their brokerage accounts to their credit or debit cards, and each of their everyday purchases is rounded up to the next whole dollar, so those cents are invested in the portfolios they selected when they set up their accounts.

People considering investing via roboadvisors can explore the options offered by companies like Wealthfront, Betterment, Fidelity Go, and Axos Invest, among others. M1 Finance and Sofi Invest also offer automated investing without charging management fees.

For investors wondering if the stockbrokers they are considering are legitimate financial services providers, this can be checked by verifying their registration status at https://brokercheck.finra.org, which includes individuals and companies.

When evaluating a stockbroker, it is also important to verify that the company is a member of the Securities Investor Protection Corporation (SIPC), which protects customers of SIPC-member broker dealers if the firm were to fail financially. SIPC membership can be verified at https://www.sipc.org/list-of-members. The value of the stocks and other securities held with a stock brokerage company, however, is not covered by SIPC. For additional information about what may be covered, investors can visit SIPC's website [Link: www.sipc.org/for-investors/what-sipc-protects].

Opening a Brokerage Account

After selecting a stockbroker company, the next step is to open an account with them. The process is similar to opening an online bank account. After filling out the paperwork and having their identity verified, people can transfer money to their accounts, explore the tools and resources available in the broker's online platform or app, research what stocks to trade, and start placing buy orders.

There are different types of accounts. For most investors, the default would be an individual brokerage account. However, there are also other types, such as joint tenants with rights of survivorship, tenancy in common, and community property. There are also custodial accounts, like those opened for minors that are transferred to the beneficiaries once they reach adulthood.

Most investors will operate with a cash account, which means that they will only be able to trade with the money they deposited into their brokerage accounts. However, investors may be also asked if they want to open a margin account. Margin is not recommended for beginning investors, since borrowing money to invest involves significantly higher levels of risk to their investment capital, so not having the ability to use margin can avoid such risk.

Investors planning to use options as part of their investment strategy could select level 2 access, which will offer them the ability to buy option calls and option puts. However, if new investors do not feel confident with options, they can decline this feature, particularly since that ability could be added at a later time, once they have improved their understanding of this instrument.

If the stockbroker offers interest on the account holders' uninvested cash, investors may be asked to select how they prefer that interest to be handled from the available alternatives. Some investors may also want to activate the option to reinvest the dividends they receive.

ORDER TYPES

The type of orders used to execute a stock trade can make a difference in the price at which that order is filled. The basic types of orders offered by stockbrokers are explained next.

- **Market Orders**. These orders get filled immediately at the best available price at the time the order is executed, but traders do not have control of the actual prices at which these orders are filled, which are likely to be different from the ones that were last quoted. To prevent substantial price differences between these two moments, some stockbrokers convert market orders to limit orders if the variation exceeds certain safety margins.

- **Limit Orders**. In this type of order, traders specify the maximum price they are willing to pay to buy a stock, or the minimum amount they are willing to receive to sell a stock. If the market prices do not reach those specified amounts, such orders are not filled. When buying, if the market price of a stock is lower than the maximum amount specified, the order will be filled at that lower market price. When selling, if the market price is higher than the minimum amount specified, the order will be filled at that higher market price.

- **Stop Orders**. Also known as stop loss orders, this type of order allows traders to define a fixed price at which a market order is activated. When placing a stop order to sell a stock, traders set a price below its current market price, and if the price of the stock drops to that level or below, then a market order to sell that stock is executed. When buying, traders set a price above its current market price, and if the price of the stock reaches that level or goes above it, then a market order to buy that stock gets executed.

- **Stop Limit Orders.** These orders allow traders to define a fixed price at which a limit order is activated. When selling a stock with a stop limit order, traders set a price below its current market price, and if the price of the stock drops to that level or below, then a limit order to sell that stock at the selected fixed price is activated. When buying with stop limit orders, traders set a price above the current market price of the stock, and if that price gets to that level or above, then a limit order to buy that stock at the selected fixed price becomes active.

Orders have attributes as well. Traders can choose the duration of their orders, with the option to have them canceled at the end of the trading day (good for day), or leave them open for a longer period, such as sixty or ninety days. They can also choose to keep their orders open only during regular trading hours, or have them remain open during extended hours as well.

Active orders can be canceled before they are executed. Some stockbrokers allow the option to edit open orders, while others require that orders be canceled and then replaced with new ones.

Traders can also specify if they want to have the full amount of their order filled (all or none) when they do not want their order to be executed in partial installments. This can be useful when purchasing large amounts of stocks using market orders, which have higher chances that such orders will be filled through several batches, each of them purchased at a different price.

If the stockbroker offers the option, investors can also have their orders filled immediately in their entirety or canceled if unable to do so (kill or fill), or have part of their orders filled immediately and cancel the parts of the order that were not filled (immediate or cancel).

Many stockbrokers allow investors to buy and sell not only whole shares but fractional ones as well. Some also give investors the option to specify dollar amounts instead of number of shares.

Investors can also set up recurring investments to buy stocks and other securities based on a prearranged schedule, such as on a daily, weekly, biweekly, or monthly basis.

Advanced Orders

As investors become more experienced, some of them may want to place more complex orders, combine orders, or use riskier trading techniques. Some of these techniques are briefly explained next.

- **Trailing Stop Orders.** This type of order allows investors to track the price of a stock as long as it moves in a favorable direction, and triggers a market order when the price of the stock moves in the opposite direction by a given percentage or dollar amount. When selling stocks with a trailing stop order, the price of the stock will be followed as long as it keeps increasing, and will only trigger a sell market order once the stock price reverses its course and has decreased by a set percentage or amount below its highest price. When buying stocks with a trailing stop order, the price of the stock will be followed as long as it keeps decreasing, and will only trigger a buy market order once the stock price reverses its course and has increased by a set percentage or amount above its lowest price. Some stockbrokers also offer trailing stop limit orders, which make the trailing orders turn into limit orders instead of market orders once their conditions are triggered and they become active.

- **Bracket Orders.** These types of orders involve a primary order to trade a stock at a given price, which is accompanied by two additional orders in the opposite direction, one higher and one lower than the primary order. For example, if an investor expects that the price of a stock will go up, they can place a primary limit order to buy it at $100, which at the same time could be bracketed by a stop order to sell it at $98 if its price were to go down, and by a limit order to sell it at $105 if the price were to go up. Once either of these sell orders is executed, the other sell order will be removed, defining a situation where once cancels the other (OCO). These orders are also referred to as three-legged orders or multiple-legged orders.

- **Short Selling.** This type of order is used by traders who expect the price of a stock to go down, so they borrow stocks from their stockbrokers, as margin transactions, and sell them at the current price, with the expectation that if their price goes down, they can purchase them at that lower price and return the borrowed stock, making a profit from that price differential. These are risky transactions, particularly if the price of the borrowed stocks increases instead of going down, since there is no limit to how much the price of stocks could go up. Accordingly, these types of orders are generally not recommended for beginning investors.

INVESTMENT PLAN

After considering the information discussed in the previous chapters and sections, investors could benefit from preparing an investment plan that puts all those different elements together and guides investors' activities in a manner consistent with their investment strategy.

Since the circumstances of each investor are unique, it is important that their investment plans reflect their own situation and risk-tolerance levels. This section includes some basic considerations to take into account when developing such a plan, criteria to consider in the definition of asset allocation, and information on guiding questions that can help investors remember key areas to look at when considering to buy, hold, or sell stocks.

Basic Considerations

Investors could benefit from assessing how much disposable income they have. This refers to the money they have left after paying their bills, monthly expenses, and other known commitments. An investment plan could also benefit from considering the source of the funds needed to invest, and ways to optimize their availability, such as deferring certain expenses, canceling some services of limited value, selling unproductive equipment, or exploring sources of secondary income.

Many investors also set aside an amount as an emergency fund, somewhere between three and six months of regular expenses, through cash or other means that can provide rapid liquidity. This fund could be helpful, for instance, to cover sudden unemployment periods without having to be forced to sell their stocks, particularly if those unforeseen events happen at times when the stock market is down.

Investors may also consider the following factors when developing their investment plans:

- **Defining an investment horizon.** The stock market may rally, drop, reverse its trend, or move sideways, but this is difficult to anticipate. However, stocks held for periods of four years or longer are more likely to experience gains. It's important to decide on the appropriate circumstances to close those positions in advance.

- **Understanding risk tolerance.** This determination can help investors remain within the parameters of their investment plans, particularly if this exercise is done before they start to invest. A realistic assessment can put things into perspective and help prevent many people from investing in more aggressive ways than what their situation would warrant.

- **Including risk management measures.** The adoption of measures to manage the risks to their portfolios is something investors should consider when preparing their investment plans, since such measures can help them weather the fluctuations of their planned investments.

- **Adopting a forward-looking approach.** While no one knows what our economy and society will look like in the future, identifying industries and companies with the potential to be market leaders in years to come may be worth exploring as possible long-term investments.

- **Doing research.** The analysis of market data is key to identifying suitable companies to invest in. This may include reading the reports and recommendations from financial analysts, identifying patterns in charts through technical analysis, reading news and interviews with experts, and reviewing the fundamentals of a company, along with other qualitative factors.

- **Creating a watchlist.** Once investors have found some stocks that fit their investment criteria, they may choose to track how the stocks perform during a given period. If the prospects look favorable, the stocks may be considered as candidates for purchasing when funds become available.

- **Sticking to their plan.** A common mistake many investors make is getting into or jumping out of the market as a reaction to their market anxiety, or other emotions leading to rash decisions, without following a plan. Even during the crisis of 2008, investors that could afford to stay in the market and resisted the urge to cash out ended up coming out ahead within eighteen months or so.

Asset Allocation

Defining the proportion in which different types of assets are allocated in a portfolio is a crucial part of an investment plan, and a key risk management measure. The three main areas whose proportions are normally considered when defining an asset allocation are stocks, bonds, and cash.

On the stock/bond ratio, an example of an asset allocation recommended by John Bogle, founder and chief executive of the Vanguard Group, is that younger investors could allocate 80 percent to stocks, preferably in the form of low-cost index funds, and 20 percent to bonds, with these proportions changing to 70 percent in stocks and 30 percent in bonds for older investors, while also considering that the proportion of bonds could go as high as 40 or 50 percent for people in the post-retirement phase (2017).

According to E*Trade, a conservative asset allocation is 20 percent stocks, 70–75 percent bonds, and 5–10 percent cash; a moderate asset allocation is 60 percent stocks, 30–35 percent bonds, and 5–10 percent cash; and an aggressive asset allocation is 80–90 percent stocks, 0–15 percent bonds, and 0–5 percent cash (2019a).

Many financial websites have asset allocation calculators that can help investors define with greater precision what their recommended asset allocation would be. However, a rule of thumb that many financial specialists use to quickly assess the proportion of stocks in relation to bonds is the rule of 110, which involves subtracting the age of the person from 110, with the result indicating the percentage in equities (Frankel 2017). For instance, a person who is twenty-five years old could have a portfolio that consists of 85 percent stocks and 15 percent bonds, while a person who is fifty years old could have a portfolio with 60 percent stocks and 40 percent bonds. This rule, however, does not take into account other factors specific to each investor other than age, such as their risk tolerance, time horizon, source of income, investing knowledge and experience, and financial goals, among others.

Young investors —particularly those with high-risk tolerances, and stock market knowledge and experience— could also define a portfolio allocation with more substantial risk exposure. An example may be one that, after setting aside cash for their emergency fund, distributes a quarter of their investment capital in defensive securities, such as a combination of bonds or ETF bonds, utility ETFs, and REITs, for instance; a quarter allocated to a combination of low-cost index funds with broad market exposure, such as the S&P 500 and the Nasdaq 100, or ETFs tracking such indexes; a quarter to ETFs or funds tracking specific sectors that investors expect to experience significant growth, such as innovation, technology, or growth ETFs, for example; and a quarter to individual stocks of solid companies deemed to have strong growth prospects at acceptable levels of risk. Such a portfolio would need to be monitored and managed to make adjustments as needed.

Rebalancing a portfolio may also be important for investors that want to maintain the same allocation of assets across different categories. For instance, if the market has gone up and the percentage of the portfolio value is now significantly more dominated by stocks, then investors could sell some of those stocks and buy other types of securities, such as bonds or ETFs. This approach would limit the growth potential of those stocks but can help maintain the resilience of a portfolio.

The key point to remember is that investment portfolios that ignore or diminish the importance of the risks associated with their asset allocations would be the ones at greater peril.

Guiding Questions

While many factors influence investors' decisions to own certain stocks and not others, and those may vary according to the specific circumstances at any given time, in many cases it may be helpful for investors to develop an abbreviated list of topics or guiding questions, to make sure they are not forgetting to check something that may be relevant to their decision.

That list of topics depends on each investor's perception of what is important to look at in stocks before making a decision to wait, purchase, hold, or sell stocks. Examples of questions that could be included in such a list are included below.

- Are the economic and socio-political trends in the country likely to favor or affect the long-term performance of the stock, and/or the economic sector in which the company operates?
- What has been the performance of the stock in the last few years (i.e., five-year chart)?
- Is the company a market leader in its niche? Are the current levels of growth likely to be sustained over time, and is the business doing something to gain a greater market share?
- What are the current market trends reflected in the major stock indexes? And are there technical indications of potential trend shifts in the market or in the price of the stock?
- Do the fundamental indicators like P/E, EPS, and debt indicate potential overpricing? If so, is there still room for substantial growth, enough to make sense to purchase it?
- If the company issues regular dividends, are they expected to remain or change over time, given the

expected position of the company in the market in relation to its competitors?

- What is the company's ESG rating and its main ESG risks? Does the company rely on manufacturing or production processes in countries that could pose challenges to its business model?
- How long is the stock planned to be kept before considering selling it? And, once bought, under what circumstances could this stock be sold before its planned time frame?

Having an exit plan for the stocks considered for purchase is in many cases as important as the criteria guiding the decision to buy them. Defining the timing and/or circumstances when the stocks could be sold can prevent investors from making rash emotional decisions.

Final Words

The price of stocks in the market fluctuates all the time, ultimately driven by supply and demand, as part of the constant movement created by the aggregated behavior of investors. New investors who adopt a long-term approach to investing, and include measures to manage the risks to their portfolios, would have a good chance of seeing their money grow over time.

The barriers to start investing in the stock market are low. Many stockbrokers allow people to open brokerage accounts for free and start investing with only one dollar. This allows investors to start participating in the stock market and gain practical experience in the way it works. The earlier they start investing, the better their chances to see significant growth in their investments.

To experience more substantial gains, however, investors could benefit from adopting habits that limit their regular expenses and increase their disposable income, which can allow them to grow their investment capital. As Stanley and Danko explained, households that kept their expenses low and were consistently able to invest part of their income were more financially resilient and able to achieve substantially higher levels of net worth over time (2010).

Knowledge of how the stock market works is one of the most important things for investors to improve their chances of being successful in the stock market. The information provided in this book, along with that available from other resources, may be used as investors see fit, since it is the way they use that information that will ultimately shape the effectiveness of their strategies.

As with many other things in life, theory is often not enough to develop the necessary skills to be successful in a consistent manner. Practice will help investors hone their ability to invest and manage risk, particularly if they adopt the habit of drawing lessons from their own experiences.

You have now reached the end of the book. I hope the information presented here can help you get started on a solid footing and prosper in your investment journey. I would love to hear what you think of this book, so please take a moment to leave a review, even a short one. It may help someone else decide that they, too, can benefit from reading it. I hope to eventually learn about your success in the stock market as well.

REFERENCES

Anderson, Stuart
2020 "Trump's Trade War Cost U.S. Company Stock Prices $1.7 Trillion." *Forbes*. Available at: https://www.forbes.com/sites/stuartanderson/2020/06/01/trumps-trade-war-cost-us-company-stock-prices-17-trillion

Bankrate
2021 "Best CD Rates." Available at: https://www.bankrate.com/banking/cds/cd-rates
2021 "Best Online Savings Accounts." Available at: https://www.bankrate.com/banking/savings/rates

Baye, Michael and Jeffrey Prince
2017 *Managerial Economics and Business Strategy*. Ninth edition. New York: McGraw-Hill

BBC
2011 "US Loses AAA Credit Rating After S&P Downgrade." Available at: https://www.bbc.com/news/world-us-canada-14428930

Binance
2020 "The Wyckoff Method Explained." Available at: https://academy.binance.com/en/articles/the-wyckoff-method-explained

Blanton, Thomas
2018 "Do Consumer Boycotts Affect Stocks?" *Kiplinger*. Available at: https://www.kiplinger.com/article/investing/t052-c000-s002-do-consumer-boycotts-affect-stocks.html

BLS
2021 Consumer Price Index: 2020 in Review. US Bureau of Labor Statistics. Available at: https://www.bls.gov/opub/ted/2021/consumer-price-index-2020-in-review.htm

Bodie, Zvi, Alex Kane, and Alan Marcus
2018 Investments. Eleventh edition. New York: McGraw-Hill

Bodner, Jason and Lucas Downey
2020 "The Market Answer Key: Big Money." *MapSignals*. Available at: https://mapsignals.com/wp-content/uploads/2020/10/The-Market-Answer-Key.pdf

Bogle, John
2017 *The Little Book of Common Sense Investing: The Only Way to Guarantee Your Fair Share of Stock Market Returns.* Second edition. Hoboken, NJ: Wiley & Sons

Bond, Casey
2019 "Here's What it Takes for a Boycott to Work." *Huffpost.* Available at: https://www.huffpost.com/entry/do-boycotts-work_l_5d4cb97be4b0066eb70f19fa

Brown, Joshua and Brian Portnoy, ed.
2020 *How I Invest My Money: Finance Experts Reveal How They Save, Spend, and Invest.* Petersfield, UK: Harriman House

Buchholz, Katharina
2020 "China Could Overtake the US as the World's Largest Economy by 2024." *World Economic Forum.* Available at: https://www.weforum.org/agenda/2020/07/largest-global-economies-1992-2008-2024

Buffett, Warren
2016 *Berkshire Hathaway Letters to Shareholders.* Compiled by Max Olson. Mountain View, CA: Explorist Productions
2008 "Buy American. I Am." *New York Times.* Available at: https://www.nytimes.com/2008/10/17/opinion/17buffett.html

Buffett, Warren and Lawrence Cunningham
2015 *The Essays of Warren Buffett: Lessons for Corporate America.* Fifth edition. Durham NC: Carolina Academic Press

Cancialosi, Chris
2017 "Preserving a Culture People Love as Your Company Grows: Lessons from Zappos." *Forbes.* Available at: www.forbes.com/sites/chriscancialosi/2017/05/30/preserving-a-culture-people-love-as-your-company-grows-lessons-from-zappos

Carter, John
2012 *Mastering the Trade: Proven Techniques for Profiting from Intraday and Swing Trading Setups.* Second edition. New York: McGraw-Hill

Chen, James
2019 "Market Capitalization." *Investopedia.* Available at: https://www.investopedia.com/terms/m/marketcapitalization.asp

Collinson, Patrick
2020 "Ethical Investments are Outperforming Traditional Funds." *The Guardian*. Available at: www.theguardian.com/money/2020/jun/13/ethical-investments-are-outperforming-traditional-funds

Cramer, Jim
2018 "Jim Cramer's 25 Rules for Investing." *The Street.* Available at: https://www.thestreet.com/files/m/white-paper/sb-72/prrg-0026_white_paper.pdf

Degnarain, Nishan
2020 "What Canada Is Getting Right with Its Covid-19 Economic Response Plan." *Forbes.* Available at: www.forbes.com/sites/nishandegnarain/2020/05/19/what-canada-is-getting-right-with-its-covid-19-economic-response-plan

Denson, Jessica
2019 "Telecommuting Could Save $700b Yearly Across the US." *Connected Nation*. Available at: https://connectednation.org/blog/2019/09/24/new-data-telecommuting-could-save-700b-yearly-across-the-us

Derousseau, Ryan
2018 "Why 'Good Guy' Stocks Can Help You Beat the Market." *Fortune.* Available at: https://fortune.com/2018/08/22/stocks-esg-arabesque-ti-cummins

Deter, Amber
2020 "TikTok IPO: Will ByteDance Go Public in 2020?" *Investment U*. Available at: https://investmentu.com/tiktok-ipo-will-bytedance-go-public-in-2020

Edwards, Robert and John Magee
2010 *Technical Analysis of Stock Trends.* Hawthorne, CA: BN Publishing

E*Trade
2019 "The Short-Selling Challenge." Available at: https://us.etrade.com/knowledge/library/perspectives/daily-insights/short-selling-challenge
2019a "Intro to asset allocation." E*Trade in collaboration with BlackRock. Available at: https://us.etrade.com/knowledge/library/getting-started/intro-to-asset-allocation

Farley, Alan
2020 "Making Money the Wyckoff Way (CSC, DNR)." *Investopedia.* Available at: https://www.investopedia.com/articles/active-trading/070715/making-money-wyckoff-way.asp

Fiegerman, Seth
2019 "Amazon Cancels Plans to Build New York Headquarters." *CNN.* Available at: https://www.cnn.com/2019/02/14/tech/amazon-hq2-nyc/index.html

Frankel, Matthew
2017 "Here's How to Determine Your Ideal Asset Allocation Strategy." *The Motley Fool.* Available at: https://www.fool.com/retirement/2017/05/28/heres-how-to-determine-your-ideal-asset-allocation.aspx

Fung, Brian
2021 "The Real Shock of the GameStop Mania was That it Didn't Happen Sooner." *CNN.* Available at: https://www.cnn.com/2021/01/28/tech/gamestop-social-media/index.html

Giddens, Anthony
1984 *The Constitution of Society: Outline of the Theory of Structuration.* Berkeley: University of California Press

Glassman, James
2020 "Investing in Uncertain Times." *Kiplinger's Personal Finance*, Dec. 2020 (32–34).
2011 *Safety Net: The Strategy for De-Risking Your Investments in a Time of Turbulence.* New York: Crown Business

Graham, Benjamin
1986 *The Intelligent Investor.* Fourth edition. New York: HarperBusiness

Greenblatt, Joel
2010 *The Little Book That Still Beats the Market.* Hoboken, NJ: John Wiley & Sons

Hayes, Adam
2020 "Value Investing." *Investopedia.* Available at: www.investopedia.com/terms/v/valueinvesting.asp

HBO
2019 *The Inventor: Out for Blood in Silicon Valley.* HBO Documentary Films. Available at: https://www.hbo.com/documentaries/the-inventor-out-for-blood-in-silicon-valley

Howe, John
2004 *The End of Fossil Energy.* Norway, ME: McIntire Publishing

Kay, John and Mervyn King
2020 *Radical Uncertainty: Decision-Making Beyond the Numbers.* New York: Norton & Company

Keegan, Paul
2015 "Here's What Really Happened at That Company That Set a $70,000 Minimum Wage." *INC.* Available at: https://www.inc.com/magazine/201511/paul-keegan/does-more-pay-mean-more-growth.html

Klock, Mark
2016 "Do Class Action Filings Affect Stock Prices? The Stock Market Reaction to Securities Class Actions Post PSLRA." *Journal of Business & Securities Law*, Vol. 15 (2):3

Krantz, Matthew
2016 *Fundamental Analysis for Dummies.* Hoboken, NJ: Wiley & Sons

Kratter, Matthew
2019 *A Beginner's Guide to the Stock Market: Everything You Need to Start Making Money Today.* Boulder, CO: Little Cash Machines LLC

Likos, Paulina
2020 "How to Pick Stocks: 7 Things All Beginner Investors Should Know." *US News.* Available at: https://money.usnews.com/investing/investing-101/slideshows/how-to-pick-stocks-things-all-beginner-investors-should-know

Lynch, Peter and John Rothchild
2000 *One Up On Wall Street: How To Use What You Already Know To Make Money In The Market.* Second edition. New York: Simon & Schuster
1996 *Learn to Earn: A Beginner's Guide to the Basics of Investing and Business.* New York: Simon & Schuster

Malkiel, Burton
2016 *A Random Walk Down Wall Street: The Time-Tested Strategy for Successful Investing.* Eleventh edition. New York: Norton & Company

Mashayekhi, Rey
2020 "A Disputed Election Could Cost the U.S. Its 'AAA' Credit Rating." *Fortune.* Available at: https://fortune.com/2020/10/13/2020-election-results-contested-us-credit-rating-aaa-peaceful-transfer-power

Maverick, J.B.
2020 "Intrinsic Value vs. Current Market Value: What's the Difference?" *Investopedia.* Available at: https://www.investopedia.com/ask/answers/011215/what-difference-between-intrinsic-value-and-current-market-value.asp

McAllen, Fred
2012 *Charting and Technical Analysis.* Dallas, TX: McAllen

Murphy, John
1999 *Technical Analysis of the Financial Markets: A Comprehensive Guide to Trading Methods and Applications.* New York: Penguin Group

New York Times
2020 "Stocks Surge as Virus Slows in Some Areas." *New York Times.* Available at: https://www.nytimes.com/2020/04/06/business/coronavirus-stock-market-live.html

Nickelsburg, Monica
2019 "Apple's Supreme Court Setback Could Spell Trouble for Other Tech Companies Facing Antitrust Scrutiny." *GeekWire.* Available at: https://www.geekwire.com/2019/apples-supreme-court-defeat-spell-trouble-tech-companies-facing-antitrust-scrutiny

Olenickjun, Doug
2015 "Does Replacing a CEO Help or Hurt a Company's Stock Price?" *The Street.* Available at: www.thestreet.com/opinion/does-replacing-a-ceo-help-or-hurt-a-companys-stock-price-13185166

O'Neil, William
2009 *How to Make Money in Stocks: A Winning System in Good Times and Bad.* Fourth edition. New York: McGraw-Hill Education

Overby, Brian
2009 *The Options Playbook.* Second edition. Fort Lauderdale, FL: TradeKing

Pant, Paula
2019 "Multiply Your Money with This Simple Rule of Thumb." *The Balance.* Available at: https://www.thebalance.com/triple-your-money-with-this-simple-rule-of-thumb-453923

Payne, David
2021 "Inflation: Gasoline Prices Drive a Bump." *Kiplinger,* updated January 13. Available at: www.kiplinger.com/economic-forecasts/inflation

Pring, Martin
2014 *Technical Analysis Explained. The Successful Investor's Guide to Spotting Investment Trends and Turning Points.* New York: McGraw-Hill Education

Pruitt, Stephen and Monroe Friedman
1986 "Determining the Effectiveness of Consumer Boycotts: A Stock Price Analysis of Their Impact on Corporate Targets." *Journal of Consumer Policy,* Vol. 9 (375–387)

RBC
2012 "Does Socially Responsible Investing Hurt Investment Returns?" *RBC GAM.* Available at: https://funds.rbcgam.com/_assets-custom/pdf/RBC-GAM-does-SRI-hurt-investment-returns.pdf

Rhea, Robert
1932 *The Dow Theory: An Explanation of Its Development and an Attempt to Define Its Usefulness as an Aid in Speculation.* New York: Barron's

Rockefeller, Barbara
2020 *Technical Analysis for Dummies.* Hoboken, NJ: Wiley & Sons

Ross, Stephen, Randolph Westerfield, and Bradford Jordan
2019 *Fundamentals of Corporate Finance.* Twelfth edition. New York: McGraw-Hill

Schwager, Jack
1999 *Getting Started in Technical Analysis.* New York: John Wiley & Sons

Sears, Steven
2019 *The Right Way to Hedge Stocks.* Barron's, Vol. XCIX(43):M9

Smith, Anne Kates
2020 "Where to Invest in 2021." *Kiplinger's Personal Finance.*

Soros, George
2003 *The Alchemy of Finance.* Hoboken, NJ: John Wiley & Sons

Stanley, Thomas and William Danko
2010 *The Millionaire Next Door: The Surprising Secrets of America's Wealthy.* Lanham, MD: Taylor Trade Publishing

Steenbarger, Brett
2002 *The Psychology of Trading: Tools and Techniques for Minding the Markets.* Hoboken, NJ: John Wiley & Sons

Stevens, Pippa
2019 "Your Complete Guide to Investing with a Conscience, a $30 Trillion Market Just getting Started." *CNBC.* Available at: https://www.cnbc.com/2019/12/14/your-complete-guide-to-socially-responsible-investing.html

Stewart, Phil
2019 "Microsoft Beats Amazon for Pentagon's $10 Billion Cloud Computing Contract." *Reuters.* Available at: https://www.reuters.com/article/us-pentagon-jedi-idUSKBN1X42IU

Swartz, Jon
2020 "Facebook Hit with Antitrust Suits that Seek to 'Unwind' Instagram, WhatsApp Acquisitions." *MarketWatch.* Available at: https://www.marketwatch.com/story/facebook-hit-with-antitrust-suit-from-ftc-and-48-states-targeted-at-acquisitions-11607543049

Tharp, Van
2006 *Trade Your Way to Financial Freedom.* Second edition. New York: McGraw-Hill Education

Tillier, Martin
2016 "The Price Correlation Between Stocks and Bonds." *Nasdaq*. Available at: https://www.nasdaq.com/articles/price-correlation-between-stocks-and-bonds-2016-10-11

Turner, Toni and Gordon Scott
2013 *Invest to Win: Earn & Keep Profits in Bull & Bear Markets with the GainsMaster Approach.* New York: McGraw-Hill Education

Van Dam, Lex
2012 *How to Make Money Trading: Everything You Need to Know to Control Your Financial Future.* London: Portico

Walsh, Ben
2019 "Robo-Advisors Are Still Hot: Here's How Their Portfolios Are Performing." *Barron's.* Available at: https://www.barrons.com/articles/best-robo-advisors-based-on-portfolio-performance-51564186630

WB
2014 "Interim Guidance Note: Systematic Operations Risk-Rating Tool (SORT)." *The World Bank*. Available at: https://www.worldbank.org/content/dam/Worldbank/document/SORT_Guidance_Note_11_7_14.pdf

Wiley, Luke
2014 *The 52-Week Low Formula: A Contrarian Strategy That Lowers Risk, Beats the Market, and Overcomes Human Emotion.* Hoboken, NJ: John Wiley & Sons

Wyckoff, Richard
1925 *How I Trade and Invest in Stocks and Bonds.* New York: The Magazine of Wall Street. Available at: https://archive.org/details/cu31924031269552

Yurieff, Kaya
2018 "Snapchat Stock Loses $1.3 Billion After Kylie Jenner Tweet." *CNN*. Available at: https://money.cnn.com/2018/02/22/technology/snapchat-update-kylie-jenner/index.html

www.ingramcontent.com/pod-product-compliance
Ingram Content Group UK Ltd.
Pitfield, Milton Keynes, MK11 3LW, UK
UKHW041838190726
13854UKWH00002B/598